IMAGES
of America

GARDEN CITY
THE FIRST 150 YEARS

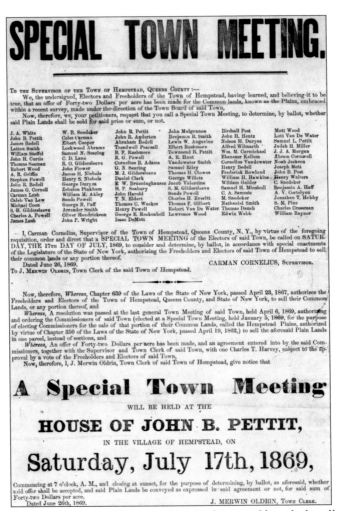

SPECIAL TOWN MEETING.

To the Supervisor of the Town of Hempstead, Queens County:—
We, the undersigned, Electors and Freeholders of the Town of Hempstead, having learned, and believing it to be true, that an offer of Forty-two Dollars per acre has been made for the Common lands, known as the Plains, embraced within a recent survey, made under the direction of the Town Board of said Town,
Now, therefore, we, your petitioners, request that you call a Special Town Meeting, to determine, by ballot, whether said Plain Lands shall be sold for said price or sum, or not.

J. A. White	W. B. Snedeker	John R. Pettit	John Mulgannon	Birdsall Post	Mott Wood
John B. Pettit	Coles Carman	John R. Appleton	Benjamin R. Smith	John H. Hentz	Lott Van De Water
James Bedell	Elbert Cooper	Abraham Bedell	Lewis W. Angevine	Nelson H. Duryea	Samuel L. Pettit
Letton Smith	Lockwood Abrams	Treadwell Pearsall	Elbert Rushmore	Alfred Wilmarth	Judah B. Miller
William Stoffel	Samuel N. Searing	B. F. Rushmore	Townsend B. Pettit	Wm. M. Carmichael	J. J. A. Morgan
John H. Curtis	C. D. Lane	R. G. Powell	A. R. Hunt	Ebenezer Kellum	Abram Cornwell
Thomas Seaman	R. O. Gildersleeve	Cornelius B. Adams	Vandewater Smith	Cornelius Vandewater	Noah Jackson
Robert Wood	John Flower	G. N. Searing	Samuel Riley	Henry Bedell	Joseph Mott
A. R. Griffin	James H. Nichols	M. J. Gildersleeve	Thomas H. Clowes	Frederick Rowland	John B. Post
Stephen Powell	Henry S. Nichols	Daniel Clark	George Willets	William H. Hawkins	Henry Walters
John R. Bedell	George Duryea	E. W. Braeninghausen	Jacob Valentine	William Golder	C. Snedeker
James G. Cornell	Zebulon Pinkham	H. P. Seabury	S. M. Gildersleeve	Samuel H. Minshull	Benjamin A. Haff
Carman Lush	William M. Akley	John Harold	Sands Powell	C. A. Sammis	A. V. Cortelyon
Caleb Van Lew	Sands Powell	T. N. Elderr	Charles H. Everitt	M. Snedeker	Jonathan T. Hebby
Michael Coon	George N. Paff	Thomas C. Weekes	Thomas F. Gilbert	Nathaniel Smith	S. M. Pine
S. H. Gildersleeve	Arrender Smith	Henry Powell	Robert Van De Water	Thomas Dauch	Charles Crossman
Charles A. Powell	Oliver Hendrickson	George E. Reckenbell	Lawrence Wood	Edwin Webb	William Raynor
James Lush	John P. Wright	Isaac DeMott			

I, Carman Cornelius, Supervisor of the Town of Hempstead, Queens County, N. Y., by virtue of the foregoing requisition, order and direct that a SPECIAL TOWN MEETING of the Electors of said Town, be called on SATURDAY, THE 17th DAY OF JULY, 1869, to consider and determine, by ballot, in accordance with special enactments of the Legislature of the State of New York, authorizing the Freeholders and Electors of said Town of Hempstead to sell their common lands or any portion thereof.
Dated June 26, 1869.   CARMAN CORNELIUS, Supervisor.
To J. Merwin Oldrin, Town Clerk of the said Town of Hempstead.

Now, therefore, Whereas, Chapter 639 of the Laws of the State of New York, passed April 23, 1867, authorizes the Freeholders and Electors of the Town of Hempstead, Queens County, and State of New York, to sell their Common Lands, or any portion thereof, and
Whereas, A resolution was passed at the last general Town Meeting of said Town, held April 6, 1869, authorizing and ordering the Commissioners of said Town (elected at a Special Town Meeting, held January 5, 1869, for the purpose of electing Commissioners for the sale of that portion of their Common Lands, called the Hempstead Plains, authorized by virtue of Chapter 350 of the Laws of the State of New York, passed April 19, 1862,) to sell the aforesaid Plain Lands in one parcel, instead of sections, and
Whereas, An offer of Forty-two Dollars per acre has been made, and an agreement entered into by the said Commissioners, together with the Supervisor and Town Clerk of said Town, with one Charles T. Harvey, subject to the approval by a vote of the Freeholders and Electors of said Town,
Now, therefore, I, J. Merwin Oldrin, Town Clerk of said Town of Hempstead, give notice that

A Special Town Meeting
WILL BE HELD AT THE
HOUSE OF JOHN B. PETTIT,
IN THE VILLAGE OF HEMPSTEAD, ON
Saturday, July 17th, 1869,

Commencing at 7 o'clock, A. M., and closing at sunset, for the purpose of determining, by ballot, as aforesaid, whether said offer shall be accepted, and said Plain Lands be conveyed as expressed in said agreement or not, for said sum of Forty-two Dollars per acre.
Dated June 26th, 1869.   J. MERWIN OLDRIN, Town Clerk.

The Beginning. With its signatories clearly visible, this historical broadside called for a day-long town meeting at the home of one John B. Pettit on July 17, 1869, to discuss Alexander Turney Stewart's offer to buy what remained of the Hempstead Plains, an area of roughly 7,000 acres. News of Garden City's future founder's all-cash $55-an-acre offer astounded local Hempstead officials, in part because they were unused to dealing in so much money: "[t]he commissioners were dazzled at the prospect of receiving such an astonishing sum for land considered worthless only a few short years before, and from a merchant prince whose limitless wealth lent authority to his words," observed Garden City historian Vincent F. Seyfried. And yet, this was only the beginning, as Stewart gave assurances to improve the land in a sensitive manner, all at his expense. The excitement only grew from there. (Garden City Village Archives Collection.)

On the Cover: Hughes Brothers, Garden City Garage, July 1946. A mainstay in Garden City during the first half of the 20th century was the Garden City Garage, whose presence helped Garden City become a modern suburban community. The garage's owners are posing alongside two of their attendants: Gerald Hughes has his hand on the gas pump, and his brother George is to his right. By the time this photograph was taken, both brothers were widely respected for their interest in community affairs. (Gerald's contribution is discussed on page 55.) Notice, however, the price they charged for a gallon of gas: 15.7¢. A simpler time, to be sure. (Garden City Village Archives Collection.)

IMAGES
of America

GARDEN CITY
THE FIRST 150 YEARS

Constantine E. Theodosiou and Emmanuel C. Theodosiou
Foreword by William A. Bellmer

ARCADIA
PUBLISHING

Published by Arcadia Publishing
Charleston, South Carolina

Printed in the United States of America

Library of Congress Control Number: 2020934620

For all general information, please contact Arcadia Publishing:
Telephone 843-853-2070
Fax 843-853-0044
E-mail sales@arcadiapublishing.com
For customer service and orders:
Toll-Free 1-888-313-2665

Visit us on the Internet at www.arcadiapublishing.com

To the memory of Alison J. Moore (1934–2013).
Wisdom is a loving spirit.

CONTENTS

FOREWORD

Everything has a history, but usually, if recorded at all, it exists in small scattered pieces. It must be brought together, often deciphered, and presented in a coherent way in order for it to be useful to the persons interested in the subject.

The Village of Garden City is fortunate to have a large source of historical material. This is due to the reason for the existence of the village: the vision of Alexander Turney Stewart, a wealthy person with the ability to implement it 150 years ago. The work he did and the effects of it over the years have always been a fascination.

Prior histories have been written that present a good picture of the evolution of the village from a largely uninhabited plain to the dense but well-organized place it is today. But the wealth of material available allows other presentations from different viewpoints. This book by Constantine Theodosiou and his son Emmanuel draws on photographs, many from the village archives, and many from diverse sources not heretofore shown as a group, to give a feeling for the people who lived, worked, were educated, or played in the area. This includes not only residents, but also those who were part of the adjacent aviation and military establishments, the public schools and Adelphi University, and those who used the three golf courses. It is a valuable addition to the historical record of the village.

William A. Bellmer
Garden City Village Historian

ACKNOWLEDGMENTS

Garden City's history, both intricate and eventful, requires care and respect. To ensure that we got our facts right and storyline straight, several people were gracious enough to lend us their expertise: Dr. Natalie Naylor, Geri Solomon, Debra Willett, Julia Lauria-Blum, Iris Levin, Erik Huber, Dr. Jeffrey Kroessler, Marjorie Freeman Harrison PhD, Marie Carella, and Jason Antos. Of course, it is not they, but the authors, who are responsible for any inaccuracies that may have found their way into the text.

We are thankful for our invaluable lifeline in the dark months of the COVID-19 pandemic, our editor Angel Prohaska, whose unwavering support was no small factor in making this book a reality.

We reserve our deepest gratitude for the gentleman who served as our friendly guide through the recesses of Garden City's past, Garden City historian William A. "Bill" Bellmer. Bill's kindness graces every page of this book, as he enabled us to compile it more easily, thoughtfully, and pleasurably than we could have ever asked for.

Any reference to Garden City's history would be remiss without acknowledging two late historians who were also Garden City residents: Mildred Smith and Vincent Seyfried. Without question, we would have loved for them to relate their knowledge of the community they cherished firsthand, but this was not meant to be. Thankfully, however, Smith's *History of Garden City*, her *Garden City, Long Island, in Early Photographs: 1869–1919*, and Seyfried's *The Founding of Garden City* all proved to be excellent resources. Along the way, we discovered John Ellis Kordes's impressive tribute to his hometown, *Visions of Garden City*. This slim yet colorful volume elegantly illustrates Garden City's genteel character from a contemporary perspective.

Many of the images were taken from three sources: the Garden City Village Archives Collection (GCVAC), the Cradle of Aviation Museum (COAM), and the Nassau County Department of Parks, Recreation and Museums Photo Archive Center (NCDP). We were also fortunate to draw upon the Jason D. Antos collection (JDA), of which the owner, a good friend, was kind enough to avail us. The authors' collection accounts for the rest.

INTRODUCTION

Lighting a candle or planting a memorial garden. Volunteering for a worthy cause. Donating to a charity on our behalf: These are but a few anodyne measures that honor our memory after we die. Each reassures our bereaved that our life is not over but rather has entered a new, if utterly mysterious, phase. A touch of immortality? We like to think so.

However, as is their wont, the socially prominent see their mortality differently. To be sure, they would welcome the tributes offered by their immediate circles, but these (one assumes) are a given. What is not is the kind of approval only posterity can give. The last and quite possibly most coveted of their earthly desires, failure to attain it in itself scuttles their posthumous reputations. To avert this, these individuals seek to impart legacies meant to endure and for the common good. "If we are to influence events after we are dead, it can only be via mechanisms that we have set up during life," observed the philosopher Geoffrey Scarre. But, more tellingly: "Some people are keener than others to make their mark on a remote posterity . . . because they think that oblivion is a threat to the meaningfulness of their lives."

This view was not lost on our protagonist. An Irish immigrant turned dry goods magnate, he was lauded for eschewing the baser profitmaking methods in New York City's business world during his prime. Years later, however, he started believing that it was incumbent upon him as a member of the city's patrician class to direct his wealth to the benefit of ordinary people, and that history demanded nothing less. For this purpose, he spared no expense in building a utopian community on Long Island—at the heart of present-day Nassau County—to offer spiritual sustenance to its future residents. Far removed from the muscular type of philanthropy that suited his contemporaries just fine, this venture was in keeping with his religious nature.

But fate cruelly denied our hero the satisfaction of seeing it come to fruition. Were it not for his widow, it would have dissolved completely, and with it, any meaningful recollection of their storied lives. Today, this important couple would be hard-pressed to identify their beloved village, save for a few structures that speak to their vision and refinement. But its place in history, their shared legacy, is no less secure for this. Hence this book.

THE STEWART LEGACY

In the antebellum years, New York City thrived. Three titans of business led the way: one was William B. Astor, whose extensive holdings led Gotham citizens to think of him as the city's landlord. After Cornelius Vanderbilt scored big in the steamboat business, he presided over a railroad empire that changed the physical landscape and social development in this country. Both men had worldviews that were to be respected; as individuals, however, they were unloved.

Not forgiven, nor forgotten, was the brash, self-interested nature of their transactions in years past. To make amends (and thus curry history's favor), both men executed a string of impressive civic projects. Astor's included completing the New York Public Library's main branch that his father, John Jacob Astor, started. Vanderbilt founded the now prestigious university that bears his name, among many other initiatives. But, as far-reaching as their legacies were, their motives and mindset will always be at issue.

The third member of the triumvirate stands as the least well known: Alexander Turney Stewart (1803–1876). Having arrived at these shores from Lisburn, northern Ireland, in 1818 to settle into a teaching career, Stewart was soon enthralled by New York City's take on the free-enterprise system. By a quirk of fate, he was able to collect his grandfather's inheritance shortly thereafter, a tidy sum he spent on bundles of Irish lace and similar finery. He then had these shipped back to New York, at which point he set up shop.

From there, Horatio Alger could not have penned a better storyline. Stewart was the first retailer in history to hold fire and remnant sales, the first to adhere to a one-price system—there would be no haggling in Mr. Stewart's store—and, amazingly, the first to stock his wares in an orderly and systematic fashion. Stewart took pains to know what the public, women in particular, found appealing, and when tending to their desires, he was always the gentleman. All this earned him a loyal following, even though he opened his storefronts in the farther reaches of Lower Manhattan. Stewart figured that if his customers made the trip just to arrive at his store, they would be determined to maximize their shopping experience. In time, he was the proud head of the Iron Store, which opened in 1862 with 2,000 people in its employ, the precursor to the modern-day department store. A.T. Stewart & Co. boasted a worldwide presence and lent its founder a dignified sobriquet: The Merchant Prince.

Stewart, a retiring man by nature, nevertheless basked in his public stature. President-elect Ulysses S. Grant, recalling how readily the Merchant Prince furnished Union troops with clean, crisp uniforms, offered him the cabinet post of treasury secretary. (Stewart reluctantly declined.) Although Stewart was known to be reserved as far as philanthropy was concerned, he saw fit to commission a grand hotel exclusively for working women. But, thanks to his friend John Kellum, he soon found his real purpose in the rural outskirts of what was then Queens County east of Manhattan.

Stewart's last-minute, all-cash offer to purchase the vestiges of the Hempstead Plains at $55 an acre—eclipsing the $42 offer already on the table—caused a stir. The land was hardly scenic, but its location was ideal for "a community for upscale working and professional people to live . . . [with] parks, streets, comfortable homes, and a commuter railroad . . . meant [for those with] . . . refined or cultivated tastes [yet] willing to live a disciplined life." The community Stewart envisaged, described by the Long Island historian William Pelletreau as a "little republic,"

> would be far enough away from New York to keep away excursion parties, its land should be common property and should not be sold outright, and even the houses would be built . . . and only leased to the settlers. It would be a complete community within itself; it would make and enact its own laws, have a large hotel capable of accommodating the most refined travelers, wide streets, superb schools, and . . . modern improvements. . . . Everything would be hedged about with restrictions, the place would be exclusive and refined—a veritable Eden.

Some were quick to deride the purchase as "Stewart's Folly." But never mind; for the future village of Garden City, the die was cast.

It looked as if Stewart's confidence alone could carry the day. He even incorporated his own rail line, named the Central Railroad of Long Island, in 1871, running from Long Island City to a brick factory in Bethpage, last known as the Nassau Brick Works, which he also built for the construction effort (the plant closed in 1981). But, seven years after ground was broken, Stewart's project reeled after he died suddenly from complications of a bad cold. Two years later, more distraction and delay came when the news broke that his corpse was stolen, launching a protracted sleuthing operation to find the culprits, who demanded $250,000 as ransom. (In the end, they accepted only $20,000, but whether they returned Stewart's actual remains is unknown.)

Garden City's fate fell on Stewart's attorney, Judge Henry Hilton, who was named its trustee. However, Hilton's designation proved to be misguided, as he demonstrated little interest in his late patron's project from the start. Seeing her dear Alexander's legacy on the line, Stewart's widow, Cornelia, took it upon herself to save it. She managed to persuade the Brooklyn Episcopal Diocese to relocate its seat to the sectarian campus at the heart of the village, known as Cathedral Town, with the newly finished Cathedral of the Incarnation as its centerpiece. (This is where she reinterred her husband's body, in a crypt at the cathedral mausoleum.) Although an impressive edifice, the cathedral would have been even more so had Hilton not callously altered its architectural renderings.

Cornelia Stewart's benevolence helped institute two mainstays in the community for years to come: the Cathedral School of St. Paul for boys, and the future Cathedral School of St. Mary for girls. Concomitantly, Judge Hilton's indifference reflected his cavalier handling of Stewart's estate overall. The extent of his self-dealing, of which Cornelia Stewart was in all probability kept in the dark, included reaping a windfall after he opened Stewart's women's hotel to the general public. Such actions erased Alexander Stewart from popular memory.

Garden City's fate was cast into deeper uncertainty upon Cornelia Stewart's own death in 1886. Her estate, mired in debt, had to answer to all sorts of legal claims made on it. And her will offered little direction: after bequeathing $2.5 million to close relatives (the Stewarts died childless), she assigned her nephew, Charles Clinch, and the ever-unpopular Judge Hilton co-executors to her estate. Wanting none of it, Clinch gave Hilton power of attorney and sole discretion over the estate's properties, the cathedral and village included. Angered that Hilton was still in the picture, Cornelia Stewart's heirs sued, resulting in years of litigation before a settlement was reached out of court. It gave them enough reason to celebrate, though, as it effectively ended Hilton's loathed trusteeship. For the beleaguered judge, it was just as well, since he now found himself embroiled in another controversy in Saratoga Springs.

Starting in 1893, the properties Stewart's heirs oversaw included 5,000 acres east of Clinton Road toward Bethpage, as the Hempstead Plains extended that far east on Long Island. However, 2,600 acres west of Clinton Road were to be managed by the newly formed Garden City Company. Witnessing the Long Island Railroad's growing impact on the area and anxious for development to start in earnest, it sold nearby lands to well-vetted developers. It did away with Stewart's outmoded directive that houses were only to be rented, not sold, which led to chronic vacancies and the area's fallow appearance. (One newspaper grimly described the neglected state of picket fences around some homes as "Stewart's ribs.")

Just as Garden City's identity began to crystallize, residents in the neighboring village of Hempstead protested over how Garden City was still taxed at the same rate as when Stewart bought the land. Tensions subsided after Garden City officials finally agreed to have their properties reassessed. This proved to be a blessing in disguise since it facilitated the Garden City Estates section's development in 1907 and opened the way toward the village's incorporation in 1919.

The moments leading up to incorporation were a nail-biter. A group of residents in Old Garden City—the area falling within a square mile of the original village—threatened to derail the move to incorporate by objecting to plans meant to include the entire school district, citing the tax burden to be imposed on them. Furthermore, they were worried that as long as Old Garden City was subject to the caprice of the village's more populated sections, such inequity would persist. But to C. Walter Randall, a locally prominent attorney who saw this drama unfold firsthand, what was needed was to offer Old Garden City residents a little something: "While thinking over the problems during that day, it occurred to me that if some acceptable assurance could be given to the residents of Old Garden City, their opposition to the [school district's incorporation] might be withdrawn and their cooperation secured."

What followed was a unique gentleman's accord to serve as the administrative basis for the future village's government: the Community Agreement, calling for equal representation on the village board of trustees regardless of the populations within Garden City's sections. (The Community Agreement passed its first test in 1931, when the village resolved to bring its Western Section into its fold.) Thus, 50 years after Garden City's founding in 1869, its incorporation put an official stamp on Alexander Turney Stewart's vision. As the great statesman Pericles said over 2,000 years ago, "What you leave behind is not what is engraved in stone monuments, but what is woven into the lives of others." The Merchant Prince can rest knowing that what he gave posterity indeed has.

THE STEWART LEGACY FLIES HIGH

In an impressive essay, Richard Guy Wilson points out that Alexander Turney Stewart left nothing in writing about what he foresaw Garden City as being. (That the bulk of Stewart's papers were discarded after his death—most likely Judge Hilton's doing—leaves posterity with little to reconstruct his life.) Likewise, any feelings he may have had as Garden City took shape are lost to history.

However, according to Wilson, Stewart's business savvy dictated that Garden City was "a real estate venture for which he would receive a return on his investment"—which made sense since, in terms of number, Stewart's landholdings followed only William Astor's. We know through Pelletreau that Stewart rejected the idea of homeownership, but, given Stewart's religiosity, one can picture him taking to the idea of becoming an inspired landlord.

Nevertheless, Garden City's religious foundation did not last. Early in the 20th century, galas at the Garden City Hotel and the genteel activities at local clubs made Garden City a go-to destination, despite its original intention. Construction in the future Garden City Estates section would later underscore the area's promise as a modern residential community. As Garden City became plush and more verdant, it took on the appearance of, in Wilson's words, "a suburban utopia emulating . . . the English Garden City movement." That Garden City became a mecca for golf seemed all but inevitable.

Garden City (as the last of the Hempstead Plains) figures prominently in our military history. During the Civil War, Camp Scott was established just south of the present-day village of Mineola, whose land once fell inside Garden City's boundaries. About four decades later, Camp Black trained troops for the Spanish-American War. In 1917, Camp Mills housed the Rainbow Division, comprised of regiments from parts of Greater New York, the standout being the Civil War's 69th New York Infantry of the Old Irish Brigade. After the truce took effect a year later, Camp Mills turned into a demobilization camp. During the Second World War, Mitchel Field Air Force Base, situated on former Hazelhurst Field No. 2, was the ground base for the Air Defense Command, assigned to defend cities and vital industrial sites, continental bases, and the Zone of the Interior.

Throughout the Great War, Roosevelt Field (or Aviation Field No. 1, renamed after Quentin Roosevelt, who died in air combat) accommodated the Air Service Aviation Concentration Center. But Roosevelt Field's meaning lies in how we historically view ourselves as a people.

Taking its leave on the damp morning of May 20, 1927, the *Spirit of St. Louis*, a custom-built, single-engine, high-wing monoplane, embarked on a solitary mission from Roosevelt Field to the other side of the Atlantic, where history awaited. The country wished the 25-year-old pilot Godspeed and, like an anxious parent, waited to see if he made it there in one piece.

Nicknamed both "the Lone Eagle" and "Lucky Lindy" by infatuated newsmen, Charles Augustus Lindbergh landed at Paris's Le Bourget Field at 10:22 the following night, 33½ hours and 3,625 miles later. Despite ecstatic calls from the crowd for him to emerge from his cockpit, he anxiously sought to check on his plane's condition first, futilely asking above the din if any mechanics were on hand. When he appeared, the self-effacing smile he sported electrified the scene further. History still hears the euphoria of the moment. But humanity came away from it inspired:

He is the poet of the air, whose pen,
A plane's propeller, spins new dreams for men.

Whether Lindbergh's, or Stewart's once (or twice) removed, *that's* a legacy.

THE MERCHANT PRINCE. Sculpted by artist Granville W. Carter, this bust of Alexander Turney Stewart looking toward the horizon was commissioned for Garden City's 100th anniversary in 1969. In life, Stewart harbored no illusions about himself. A retiring man by nature, he also had confidence in his own abilities, something his obituary in the *New York Times* bears out: "Stewart's life was proof of the efficacy of honesty, industry and well directed intelligence. The man who has amassed the largest fortune ever accumulated within the span of a single life was simply a hardworking, careful merchant, with a decided talent for organization and a somewhat rare faculty for taking as firm a grasp of petty details as of broad and general principles." The monument, the only one of Stewart anywhere, stands in Hubbell Plaza today.

One

FROM THE PLAINS, A CITY

RUSTIC SCENE, C. 1905. According to Mildred H. Smith, the child sitting under her grandmother's gaze is Ruth Velcor picking bird's-foot violets (*viola pedata*). While Ruth steals our attention, what is significant is the land on which she sits, being the last remnant of the Hempstead Plains (where bird's-foot violets regularly flourished). This was the territory Alexander Turney Stewart bought to create a utopian community he would call Garden City. Over time, the land's flat, treeless topography played an important role in broadening Garden City's historical importance after Stewart and his wife, Cornelia, died, in 1876 and 1886, respectively. (COAM.)

FOUNDER, GARDEN CITY. Alexander Turney Stewart (1803–1876) was an immigrant from Lisburn, Ireland, retail giant, and community founder. Through his grandfather's inheritance, Stewart opened a retail textile shop that he eventually grew into the precursor of the modern-day American department store. One of the wealthiest men in his day, Stewart was also a religious man and believed a model community would be the best way to serve the public and, by extension, how he should be remembered. Today, Garden City (a name Stewart chose because he liked the way it sounded) stands as one of Long Island's premier addresses. (GCVAC.)

KEEPER OF THE FLAME. Cornelia Clinch Stewart (1803–1886) married Alexander Stewart in 1823. After he died in 1876, she used her inheritance, a sum totaling $50 million, to keep his legacy alive, thus making it hers as well (they had no children). Her chief accomplishment was to convince the Episcopal Diocese of Brooklyn to relocate to Garden City with the completion of the Cathedral of the Incarnation, a bishop's house, deanery, and cathedral schools. Although she died in 1886 before her plans were completed, her open-handedness shaped Garden City's early and timeless character. (GCVAC.)

THE IRON STORE. From a modest storefront, A.T. Stewart expanded his business until it evolved into this massive five-story building in 1862 in Lower Manhattan, which took up an entire block at Ninth and Tenth Streets, alongside Broadway and Fourth Avenue. Referred to as the Iron Store for its cast-iron architecture (cast iron being a new construction material at the time), this building was later taken over by John Wanamaker, who merged it with his business empire after Stewart's death in 1876.

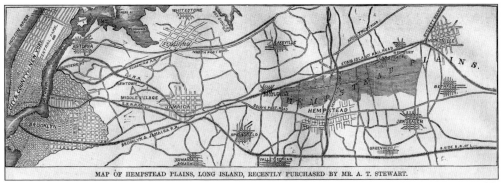

MAP OF HEMPSTEAD PLAINS, LONG ISLAND, RECENTLY PURCHASED BY MR. A. T. STEWART.

ANNOUNCING STEWART'S PURCHASE. Combined, this map and article appeared in *Harper's Weekly* on August 7, 1869, to announce the Town of Hempstead's ratification of Alexander Stewart's purchase of the Hempstead Plains. Notice how deeply the 7,000-acre acquisition goes into central Long Island and that the article is pointing out its $400,000 cost. But there is more. The article also highlights Stewart's plans "to spend from six to ten millions of dollars" to develop the land "for homes for the working-classes of New York and Brooklyn," a prospect so "gigantic that it throws into the shade of the kind hitherto made." The last third of it extols Stewart's abiding commitment to see to it that his community flourishes: "Hempstead Plains, hitherto a desert, will be made to blossom as the rose; it will be the most beautiful suburb in the vicinity of New York. God speed the undertaking!"

THE HEMPSTEAD PLAINS.

THE purchase of Hempstead Plains—a tract of land in the interior of Long Island, consisting of 7000 acres—by Mr. A. T. STEWART was ratified by the citizens of Hempstead July 17. We give on this page a very full map of this region, showing its connection by railroad with Brooklyn and New York. This tract cost Mr. STEWART $400,000; and we understand that it is his design to spend from six to ten millions of dollars in the erection upon it of homes for the working-classes of New York and Brooklyn. This design is so gigantic that it throws into the shade every attempt of the kind hitherto made. The situation of the lands purchased is admirably adapted to the purposes contemplated. They are abundantly supplied with the purest water; the Ridgewood Water-works of Brooklyn are fed by the springs of this region. As will be seen by a glance at our map, the Long Island and the Southside railroads (with a branch road connecting them, and running across the Plains) afford unusual facilities for communication with the two neighboring cities. With the improvements which Mr. STEWART will carry out; with a township of beautiful and healthful homes; with parks, gardens, and public buildings for educational purposes and for those of amusement, Hempstead Plains, hitherto a desert, will be made to blossom as the rose; it will be the most beautiful suburb in the vicinity of New York. God speed the undertaking!

JOHN KELLUM. Alexander Turney Stewart's trusted friend and architect, Kellum (1809–1871) oversaw the village of Garden City's initial development, between Rockaway Avenue and Franklin Avenue. Kellum, a former resident of Hempstead who knew its traditions and inner workings well, counseled Stewart into purchasing the Hempstead Plains. His architectural firm was responsible for several fine buildings in Manhattan, including Stewart's Fifth Avenue mansion (dubbed "the Marble Palace"), as well as the Iron Store (see page 16). As a tribute to Kellum after his death in 1871, his plans for Garden City were followed to the letter. (GCVAC.)

MEN AT WORK, C. 1911. The location of this early Garden City scene is unspecified, but that does not take away from the workers exerting themselves while paving a street in the area. Thanks to the goings-on at the Nassau Boulevard airfield at the time, Garden City's growing reputation for aviation warranted further development in the vicinity.

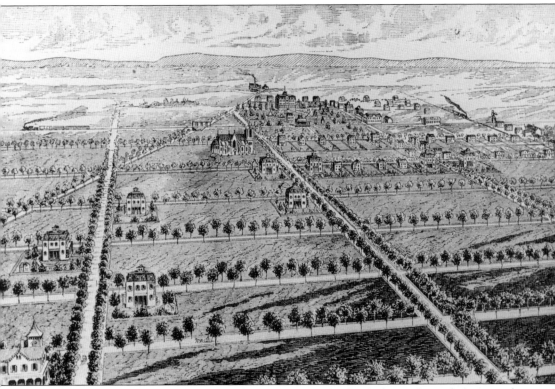

PERIOD RENDERING, MARCH 1878. According to Vincent Seyfried, this is the earliest view of Garden City. The view northward is from First Street, and Rockaway Avenue is to the left. To the right toward the center is Cathedral Avenue, with the Cathedral of the Incarnation under construction, whose spire has not yet been erected. The train at right is moving south from Mineola on its way to Hempstead and is about to cross Stewart's east-west Central Railroad of Long Island (CRRLI) line that the train on the left is on. Just to the right of that crossing is the water tower with the rotor on top (see page 29). At top center is the waterworks at Cherry Valley and Eleventh Street. (GCVAC.)

Cathedral Ave. showing Cathedral,
Garden City, L.I.

EARLY CATHEDRAL AVENUE. Garden City's appealing bucolic character is coming into its own in this undated postcard. At far left, past the approaching horse and buggy, is a sliver of the Cathedral of the Incarnation; to the right, an ethereal depiction of St. Mary's School for Girls is discernible. Both are central to Garden City's character. The trees lining the path all but guarantee serenity to anyone traveling on it.

CORNERSTONE LAYING CEREMONY, JUNE 28, 1877. This historical photograph shows the initial phase of the Cathedral of the Incarnation's construction. To the left, where crane necks are visible, the cathedral's walls and arched windows are in place. The wide tents are where the ceremony was held, and in the distance is a lengthy passenger train, three of which, according to Mildred Smith, were used to bring the day's visitors from New York and Brooklyn. (A contemporary newspaper account stated that attendance at the ceremony was in the thousands.) Note the eerie presence of "ghost" carriages thanks to the photographer's use of a lengthy exposure time. (GCVAC.)

CATHEDRAL OF THE INCARNATION. Here, in all its glory, is the centerpiece of the village of Garden City, the cruciform-decorated Gothic Cathedral of the Incarnation. Endowed by the widow Stewart, she wished it to be a memorial for her late husband, Alexander, and thus took an active interest in every phase of its construction. She used it to entice the Brooklyn Episcopal Diocese to move to Garden City, which, after some hesitancy, it did. Designed by William H. Harris and dedicated in 1885, the cathedral still holds the distinction as the only one in the country ever funded by a single person.

INTERIOR
CATHEDRAL OF THE INCARNATION
GARDEN CITY, N.Y.

HEAVENLY INTERIOR. As one steps inside the Cathedral of the Incarnation and faces its nave, what is immediately apparent is the cathedral's grand Gothic-inspired interior. Notice the slender yet ornate pillars with their adorned bases, and how their styled capitals support the magnificently pointed arches and elaborate vaulting, rising 53 feet from the floor. Its glorious stained-glass windows were commissioned in 1882 from the London-based firm of Claydon, Bell and Company. Today, the pews are permanently fixed to the floor, but other than this, the cathedral's original interior remains as it always was.

BISHOP ABRAM NEWKIRK LITTLEJOHN. Despite Cornelia Stewart's proposal to have the Cathedral of the Incarnation be the new seat of the Episcopal diocese, many Episcopal clergies in Brooklyn (the borough of churches) refused to go to Garden City, citing its isolation and that its future, given Alexander Stewart's untimely death, was uncertain. Countering them was Reverend Littlejohn (1824–1901), who believed that Cornelia Stewart's offer could, in fact, establish a "proper" diocese. Once she and Judge Henry Hilton agreed to Littlejohn's terms and conditions, opponents to the plan relented.

SEE HOUSE, OR BISHOP'S RESIDENCE. The See House was what Bishop Littlejohn called home during his Garden City ministry. Composed of 32 rooms, the structure, according to the *New York Sun*, is made of brick with free-stone trim and is four stories high. It was lavishly furnished, with mahogany woodwork from San Domingo, along with oak floors, mosaic borders of black walnut, and high ceilings from which brass lamps hung. Eclectic furnishings ran throughout. There was even a servant's quarters on the top floor, and a coachman's quarters could be found in the distance on Fourth Street.

BISHOP'S STUDY, c. 1940s. With an opulent library at the bishop's disposal, this dignified and spacious room seems to lend itself to theological contemplation. It also seems to provide the bishop with the intellectual means to reinforce his moral authority over his congregants. (GCVAC.)

LOCAL VISTA. This scene was taken from the top of the hotel facing east. Included are houses on Eighth Street (now Stewart Avenue) that were all moved to Ninth Street when it was proposed around 1915 to widen the street between Hilton and Franklin Avenues. Included are the two Apostle Houses on the east side of Hilton Avenue in the foreground that were replaced by Hilton Hall. (The north side of Seventh Street, at right, did not include the Garden City Garage at Franklin Avenue yet, dating the photograph to before 1908.) (GCVAC.)

EARLY DEVELOPER JAMES HENRY L'HOMMEDIEU.
Born in Smithtown, Suffolk County, James
H. L'Hommedieu (1833–1892) was reared on a
local farm and received only a meager formal
education. After apprenticing under his uncle,
a well-known builder, he set up a building
material business in Great Neck. Soon after,
"he designed and erected some of the most
costly and elegant residences in the country
. . . establishing a reputation second to that
of no other architect either on Long Island or
in New York City." It was at this time that he
established an amicable working relationship
with Alexander Stewart, which L'Hommedieu
would extend to Cornelia after her husband's
death. Likewise, L'Hommedieu was "responsible
for erecting every building in Garden City,
including the Cathedral of the Incarnation
. . . besides other buildings elsewhere."

APOSTLE HOUSE, 1877. Designed by John Kellum, this fine house was one of 10 built. At $18,000 each, they stood among the first and largest in the nascent village of Garden City. The graceful Second Empire design was intended to complement the area's larger edifices, the Garden City Hotel in particular, and was targeted to prospective homeowners with means. Word has it that the moniker "Apostle" came from the students of the cathedral schools, who dormed there before their buildings were completed. This photograph was taken the same day that the cornerstone of the Cathedral of the Incarnation was laid (see page 20). In fact, this house burned down due to a lightning strike, and the bishop's residence was subsequently built nearby (see page 23). (GCVAC.)

25

DISCIPLE HOUSES. Also designed by Kellum were firebrick homes such as this one at 73 Hilton Avenue adjacent to the present village hall. These Disciple Houses were more modest than the Apostle Houses, yet refined nonetheless. (And yes, their moniker also came from the Cathedral School students.) Looking a bit worse for wear in this Kodachrome picture, however, this specimen was torn down in 1960 by the Garden City village for, as a *Newsday* article put it, "no immediate purpose but 'to make room for future expansion.' " Today, the land is part of the community park at the western part of the Village Hall property, where it has the local September 11 memorial. (GCVAC.)

WORKMEN COTTAGES (C. 1870–1880). The least expensive homes built in the Garden City area were these 10 workmen's houses on the east side of Franklin Avenue, south of the railroad crossing. Originally built to house workmen (largely newly arrived Polish immigrants) who Stewart hired to build his village, these modest cottages offered enough amenities to ensure they would stay on the job until its completion. When the Doubleday publishing house bought 40 acres along Franklin Avenue for its Country Life Press division, these homes were moved to Franklin Court. They were later modernized, and today they inhabit Franklin Court West.

WATERWORKS, C. LATE 1800s. If Stewart's vision was comprehensive and ingenious, L'Hommedieu's touch was deft and sensitive. This is the village's waterworks system of the latter's design. An enchanting structure that belies its utilitarian function, it was completed in 1876 to replace wells and hand pumps throughout the village. Seated on the end of Cherry Valley Avenue and Eleventh Street six blocks north of the Cathedral of the Incarnation, this castellated structure was built to pump water through seven miles of piping to meet the needs of residents. The engineer's house (demolished in the 1950s) is to the left; to the right is the great well, named because it was 50 feet in diameter and produced water from 40 feet underground.

GARDEN CITY STATION, C. 1873. Another early structure was the village's first railroad station, whose attractive design, à la John Kellum, was deliberately done to punctuate the end of a tree-lined avenue; the building itself faced the Garden City Hotel. Together, these structures, one big and this one smaller, harmonized for a charming juxtaposition visitors would remember. A long sheltering roof extending to a platform attached to the back of the station was intended to protect passengers from the elements. The building also housed the village's first post office. (GCVAC.)

GARDEN CITY STATION WITH ESTATE OFFICE, 1873. Here, the Garden City train station is seen in a view facing west with the estate office at right, which a fire destroyed in 1911. The long sheltering roof mentioned on the previous page is visible. (NCDP.)

STEWART LOCOMOTIVE ON THE CENTRAL RAILROAD, C. 1870S. According to Mildred Smith, this engine could be the Hempstead 12 or Garden City 10, built in 1872 by the Rhode Island Locomotive Works. The Stewart-built line the train sits on was the Central Railroad of Long Island. Vincent Seyfried maintained that the CCRLI furnished Pullman Palace Car service in 1874 and provided weekend excursions to Garden City for prospective tenants to "look over the Village." (GCVAC.)

RALPH PETERS, PRESIDENT, LONG ISLAND RAILROAD.
Georgia-born railroad executive Ralph Peters
(1853–1923) fancied Garden City enough to
come to live there. Elected president of the Long
Island Railroad (LIRR) in 1905, he oversaw its
development, being particularly interested in its
potential connection with New York City's subway
system. Peters subscribed to the idea that life was a
matter of working hard and playing hard. The *New
York Times* made it clear where Garden City fit in:
"The gospel of my life has been work, hard work,
and I seem to have plenty of that here. . . . But . . .
I also love to play—when I can. I am going . . . to
Garden City for a game of golf . . . the greatest sport
ever devised for the businessman." (GCVAC.)

HEMPSTEAD CROSSING INTERLOCKING TOWER AND WATER TOWER, C. 1920. Stewart constructed
his own rail line to serve residents and visitors from the city. Running from Flushing, Queens, to
Babylon in Suffolk County, the CRRLI had two branches: one to Hempstead ending at Fulton
Street and the other to a Stewart-built brickworks in Bethpage. In Garden City, it crossed a pre-
existing LIRR line from Mineola to Hempstead. The interlocking tower in this image, called
Hempstead Crossing and located east of Franklin Avenue and north of the Country Life Press
station, controlled signals and switches for tracks providing routings between Garden City, Clinton
Road and East Mineola, Hempstead, and Valley Stream in an arrangement called a wye layout
(actually a diamond). The water tower in the back supplied steam locomotives. Both structures
were removed in 1939, along with most of the tracks at later dates. Today, the site is used for
parking, informally referred to as the Wye parking field. (GCVAC.)

Map of Central Garden City, 1891. This 1891 map in an atlas by Chester Wolverton shows the relatively few roads and buildings that constituted Garden City at the time. The original hotel is shown along with the cathedral and St. Paul's School; St. Mary's School was yet to exist on Cathedral Avenue between Fourth and Fifth Streets. A distinguishing feature of the railroad depot is that its central location is in a park, a feature missing in most other stations. The fairgrounds preceded the development of the village. The waterworks was at the head of the valley traversed by Cherry Valley Avenue. Also shown are all the existing houses at the time. The original street names honoring famous persons had been changed to the ones shown. Eighth Street subsequently became Stewart Avenue. (GCVAC.)

HOME OF LOCAL VIP. This 1908 scene is the corner of Kilburn Road east of Nassau Boulevard on Stewart Avenue. To the left is the Dutch Colonial home of former lieutenant governor Timothy Woodruff, also a founder and vice president of the Garden City Estates Corporation. Woodruff (see page 66) relished his place in the Garden City community, sponsoring (according to Mildred Smith) the community clubhouse for tennis, being an enthusiast for the local Vanderbilt car race and the Aero Club, and helping to develop the Nassau Boulevard Aerodrome west of the Estates properties. Woodruff would play a key role in the authorization for the first airmail flight to commence from there in 1911. (GCVAC.)

CATHEDRAL SCHOOL OF ST. PAUL. The first of the two cathedral schools instituted by Cornelia Stewart, St. Paul's School for Boys was dedicated in 1879 and opened in 1883 as a military boarding school. Designed by William H. Harris, who also drew the plans for the Cathedral of the Incarnation (see page 21) and later St. Mary's School, St. Paul's is a massive Victorian Gothic structure built by James L'Hommedieu. It took the shape of an "E" and had a slate roof and a clock and bell tower. With its top-notch facilities, it offered an education that befitted the scions of upper-class families who first enrolled there and the many who followed. It closed its doors in 1991, but, although landmarked, its future is cloudy largely due to the costs associated with its rehabilitation. As of this writing, there is no clear path as to its future use.

St. Paul's Parlor, c. 1880s. This interior view is the stately parlor found within St. Paul's. The furniture and gas chandeliers were from Stewart's store. (GCVAC.)

Faculty Members. This undated photograph presents a group portrait of St. Paul's faculty, with the headmaster, Dr. Frederick L. Gamage, seated at center. The names of the others are unfortunately lost. Their seriousness of purpose is apparent. (GCVAC.)

CADETS IN FORMATION, C. 1883–1893. Being cadets in a military academy, St. Paul's students had to undergo soldierly instruction. These cadets are in full dress uniform, with rifles in hand and standing at attention. In front are upperclassmen with swords, but at ease. Unfortunately, documentation for this image is lacking, so it is unknown whether this scene was part of a patriotic ceremony or a routine exercise. But notice that the American flag is carried in the back. (GCVAC.)

CANNON FIRE, C. 1880s. The right portion of this image is not obliterated, but rather obscured in a huge plume of cannon smoke as part of an artillery training exercise under the steady gaze of a US Army officer. According to John Ellis Kordes, cannons and artillery used at St. Paul's were made available by the federal government. (GCVAC.)

MARCHING BAND, C. 1890S. Standing beneath the porte-cochere (literally a "coach gateway," but here meaning a covered entranceway) on the east side of St. Paul's is a small group of lowerclassmen who comprised the school's marching band. Note their seriousness as they wait for their signal to proceed—a mark of instilled discipline. (GCVAC.)

BENJAMIN TALBOT BABBITT HYDE. A former cadet of St. Paul's, Hyde (1872–1933) was destined for bigger and better things while holding fast to the principles of his former school. After taking special courses at Harvard, Hyde eventually assumed control of his grandfather's laundry soap company. He then became a natural scientist and benefactor of the American Museum of Natural History. He was also a staunch advocate for the Boy Scouts (where he was called "Uncle Bennie") and other youth organizations. He attained a measure of local notoriety as the first to explore the ruins of the Pueblo Bonita in New Mexico's Chaco Canyon. The Hyde Memorial, a park eight miles from Santa Fe, was named in his honor. The *Encyclopedia of New Mexico* in 1945 paid tribute to Hyde: "His passing marked the close of the career of one of the most beloved and outstanding citizens of Capital City."

INFORMAL PARLOR GATHERING. This later photograph (taken perhaps in the 1930s) presents a group of well-dressed young men, most likely upperclassmen, informally gathered in the parlor of St. Paul's, by now a preeminent prep school. Judging by their appearance, St. Paul's students hailed from the social elite, which entrusted the school to give their sons the fundamentals to become leaders in medicine, law, science, divinity, and education. (GCVAC.)

CATHEDRAL SCHOOL OF ST. MARY. Also designed by William H. Harris and built by James L'Hommedieu is St. Paul's female counterpart, St. Mary's School, formerly east of Cathedral Avenue between Fourth and Fifth Streets. Opened in 1892, more than a decade after St. Paul's, the smaller St. Mary's had a similar curriculum: classes in Latin, mathematics, geography, science, and religious studies, to ensure that its charges received a well-rounded education. St. Mary's was torn down in 2001 after a fire damaged the derelict building the year before. It was a sad loss.

DRAWING ROOM, 1907. Comparable to the august parlor in St. Paul's (see page 32) is this elegant late-Victorian room in St. Mary's where visitors were received. This room, complete with plush chairs, a loveseat, and a fireplace to the left, could have been where students met to socialize. The sunlight suffusing the entire room lends it a relaxed atmosphere. (GCVAC.)

GATHERING AT ENTRANCE, C. 1900s. Standing out in this assemblage of women before the St. Mary's entrance are those dressed in the Gibson Girl fashion, which was in vogue for the younger set when this photograph was taken. Not to be overlooked are the older women in more conservative dress. (GCVAC.)

St. Mary's Basketball Team, 1910. In keeping with the time-honored idea that athleticism is essential to a sound education, St. Mary's offered sports including tennis and basketball. The woman in white at back is presumably the coach. The significance of the armbands is unknown. (GCVAC.)

Basketball Game. Caught in this undated scene is a girls' basketball game under the watchful eye of an instructor—possibly the same woman in the prior image—at right. Behind the girls is a tennis court, with a player in action. (GCVAC.)

TENNIS GROUP, 1889. Along with basketball, St. Mary's students played tennis, evidenced by this group of students of varying ages. Many are holding rackets, but one girl at left in a patterned dress seems to have chosen to hold hers as though it were a guitar. (GCVAC.)

RECITAL. In this undated photograph (possibly taken in the 1930s), a harp recital is in progress before an audience of St. Mary's students. Both schools were committed to providing a classically-inspired education. (GCVAC.)

GARDEN CITY HOTEL, C. 1880S. Seen here is the first Garden City Hotel on Seventh Street. Built by Alexander Stewart at a hefty cost of $150,000, it was situated on a 23-acre landscaped park, directly and deliberately across from the CRRLI, and accessible to local avenues and streets. Construction began in the fall of 1873, and its opening took place amid great hoopla the following summer. (GCVAC.)

GARDEN CITY HOTEL: SECOND INCARNATION, C. 1890S. Designed by McKim Mead & White (one of whose partners, Stanford White, was affiliated with the Garden City Company), this remodeled version of the Garden City Hotel made Garden City a place where the elite came to be seen. A redbrick building in the Georgian Revival style, the hotel's cupola, flying a large American flag, catches attention, as do its two graceful wings. According to Mildred Smith, the hotel "was large enough to house 200 guests . . . provided welcoming piazzas, dining rooms overlooking the gardens, handsomely furnished reception and drawing rooms and elevator service to the rooms and suites above—ten with private bathrooms." The men also took advantage of additional accoutrements. (GCVAC.)

GARDEN CITY TAXI. In this undated photograph is the Garden City taxi, a canopy-top surrey with Bert Totten at the reins. While its exact location is undetermined, it was a common sight throughout Garden City, be it near the railroad station or at the hotel, where it would be summoned to take visitors to their desired destinations. (GCVAC.)

GARDEN CITY HOTEL: THIRD INCARNATION, C. 1920s–1930s. Here is the third, and arguably the finest, incarnation of the Garden City Hotel, ensconced in the greenery Garden City would be known for. Built after a fire gutted the second hotel in 1899, this structure, also designed by McKim Mead & White, saw much of 20th-century history, greeting dignitaries including John F. Kennedy, Margaret Thatcher, Hillary Clinton, and George H.W. Bush, Saudi Arabia's Prince Khalid, and Irish prime minister Garret Fitzgerald. Due to financial difficulties and deteriorating condition, it closed in 1973 and was torn down shortly thereafter, much to the sadness of the community.

JOSEPH J. LANNIN. Canadian-born entrepreneur Joseph Lannin (1866–1928) was the proprietor of the Garden City Hotel at the time of his death. Though of limited formal education, Lannin had a keen business sense that led to, among other things, owning the Boston Red Sox and signing Babe Ruth to the team. In addition to the Garden City Hotel (one of several hotels he owned), Lannin also possessed Roosevelt Field at the time Charles Lindbergh made his historic flight to Europe. Known to have a chronic heart condition, Lannin tragically died from falling out of a window from one of his hotels in Brooklyn. Presumably, he got dizzy after trying to open it for some air.

BEFORE THE HOTEL'S ENTRANCE, 1907. Here is an intimate view of the third hotel with cabs in front and drivers patiently waiting for passengers. Clearly, the auto age had reached Garden City (the Garden City Company built a garage on Seventh Street to accommodate the vehicles of visitors). Notice some individuals taking in the sun on the veranda and some standing under the canopy at the hotel's entrance. The hotel's fine architectural details shine through. (GCVAC.)

ESTEEMED GUEST, MAY 1927. Hours before his historic flight over the Atlantic, Charles Lindbergh (right) was engaged in a possibly work-related talk in the Garden City Hotel with fellow aviator Clarence D. Chamberlain, pilot of the *Columbia*, a Bellanca monoplane. Lindy appears dressed in his aviation outfit, which stands to reason, since Roosevelt Field, where on the morning of May 20 he embarked on his groundbreaking journey, was but a short distance from the hotel (see pages 154–157). (GCVAC.)

Two

AN UPSCALE COMMUNITY

EXITING CLINTON ROAD, C. 1910S. As Nassau County became one of America's preeminent suburban counties in the 20th century, automobiles started to make themselves felt even in idyllic communities such as Garden City. While this scene of a solitary vehicle exiting the station plaza at Clinton Road captures a tranquil mood, make no mistake, the Garden City area was about to see some major changes. Cars, more than trains, would be the means by which people came to the area, either as visitors or potential homebuyers. Either way, Garden City's development took off by leaps and bounds. (GCVAC.)

ESTATE OFFICE, C. 1875. This was the estate, or manager's, office on the west side of the road between the railroad station and Seventh Street. People hoping to settle in the area either as tenants or homebuyers would have wanted to speak with W.R. Hinsdale to get a lay of the land. Built by James L'Hommedieu two years before this photograph was taken, the upper floors of this delightful structure were where important documents were kept, all of which were lost when a fire destroyed the house in January 1912.

GARDEN CITY RAILROAD STATION, C. 1900S. This uncommon view of the second (c. 1892) Garden City railroad station reveals the estate office at left. As the Garden City Company was in the midst of expanding development, it was useful and convenient for the estate office to be near the rail station. The semaphore prominently stands at center, and beneath it is a solitary individual who looks like he is waiting for the train.

ROAD GRADING, GARDEN CITY ESTATES, 1907. Among the early and crucial tasks these workmen were assigned was grading streets, as seen here. Note how both a steam engine, or perhaps an early road grader, and horse-drawn teams are used to ensure the street's levelness or to allow for drainage. (GCVAC.)

GARDEN CITY ESTATES AT NASSAU BOULEVARD, C. 1910S. This expansive scene is Nassau Boulevard looking south, with a grade crossing at far right. Prominently displayed for the benefit of incoming passengers is a large sign at center left indicating that they have reached the newly developed Garden City Estates. While an early image, the sense of refinement is becoming apparent. (GCVAC.)

NASSAU BOULEVARD TRAIN STATION, C. 1908 OR 1910. This view of Nassau Boulevard facing southwest shows the handsome Nassau Boulevard Station, built at a cost of $10,000, with its plaza and pergola amid tasteful landscaping done by A.R. Petit, who was responsible for much of the landscaping throughout Garden City in its early period. (GCVAC.)

CLINTON ROAD TRAIN STATION, POSSIBLY C. LATE 1910s. In an effort to make improvements on the rail station at Nassau Boulevard in the Estates area, Gage Tarbell had a similar station house erected for his new 1910 development in the eastern part of the village. It did not have scheduled service at first, but when Camp Mills was established nearby in 1917, it suddenly became busy, with a shuttle running between it and the Garden City station. The shuttle was subsequently rerouted to the Country Life Press station and served the new companies east of the village as well as Mitchel Field. The station was closed when the shuttle service ended in 1953 and was converted by the village to a firehouse to serve the eastern section. (GCVAC.)

GARDEN CITY

is less than 20 miles from New York, with through electric service in 35 minutes to the Pennsylvania Station and practically the same time to Wall Street. About 50 minutes by automobile.

Garden City is famous for its schools, hotel, Cathedral, golf, polo, aviation, motoring, parks and beautiful avenues.

In fact country sports and country life are here found at their best.

Its homes are most attractive and the place is without a single objectionable feature.

The climate is delightful throughout the year, the soil renowned for its fertility and the water for its purity. Improvements the very best to be found.

New modern homes for sale from $8,000 to $50,000, on terms to suit responsible buyers.

Houses for rent, furnished and unfurnished.

Choice building plots bordering on and near golf links, at excellent value.

Additional information gladly furnished

GAGE E. TARBELL
Tel. Mad. Sq. 7944, 320 Fifth Avenue, N. Y.

ADVERTISEMENT, C. 1920S. Residential development in Garden City could only go so far by word of mouth alone. In 1906, the Garden City Company sold a one square mile piece of property to the west of the St. Paul's school to an outside development company that included Gage E. Tarbell and Timothy Woodruff for $1.5 million. The developers then proceeded to build Garden City Estates in a way sensitive to Stewart's original plan. Printed advertisements such as this gained attention with photographs of attractive homes for sale and purple prose that described what living here would be like, as well as how easy the commute was to Manhattan, making Garden City appealing as a bedroom community: "Its homes are most attractive and the place is without a single objectionable feature."

DEVELOPER, GARDEN CITY ESTATES. Gage E. Tarbell (1856–1936) was in charge of developing Garden City Estates. Having grown up poor, Tarbell was a jeweler, lawyer, and even mining promoter. But it was as an insurance broker that Tarbell made his mark, eventually becoming vice president of the Equitable Assurance Company. In Garden City, where he would eventually reside, Tarbell saw to it that Garden City Estates was aimed at people with refined tastes, noted by the kind of homes illustrated in the ad on the previous page. In so doing, he crystallized Garden City as the suburban community it is known as today. (GCVAC.)

GAGE E. TARBELL'S MANSION, DEMOLISHED IN 1964. Gage E. Tarbell's full-block five-acre home on the north side of Stewart Avenue reflected both his financial success and his personal taste. In January 1910, the *New York Times* described at length what it would be like once completed: "[Its] exterior will be of solid brick walls stuccoed with white cement and the roof of blue-green tile. The balconies and the main entrance door are of iron, the ornamental walls of cast cement." The house's nicest feature were its loggias, roofed open galleries that could be enclosed in glass to be heated and occupied during the winter, "one in connection with the living room, and the other for dining purposes opening out of the main dining hall." A third loggia would later replace the servant's entrance, "thus making the house most symmetrical throughout." (GCVAC.)

GARDEN CITY ESTATES AERIAL VIEW, 1928. This view of Garden City Estates facing east (taken by Bill Ryan, US Army Air Corps) shows a substantial degree of residential development by this time. In the back is a field showing the construction of the soon-to-be-modernized Adelphi University campus. Kilburn Road and Salisbury Avenue along Nassau Boulevard are also featured, along with the Grandma Hamilton House on the northwest corner of the intersection. (GCVAC.)

GOULD RESIDENCE, C. 1920S. The owner of this still-extant fine home on the east side of the village at 401 Stewart Avenue was Maurice P. Gould, owner of a Manhattan-based company that pioneered the mass distribution of pharmaceuticals from as early as 1905. One strategy Gould's company devised to target independent drugstores was to have an advertisement with a picture of a very prominent pharmacologist who had long patronized the M.P Gould Company, signifying its importance. A coupon was included meant for the druggist to obtain the know-how to market medicinal products using a Gould-inspired method.

FRANKLIN COURT, 1912. According to Mildred Smith, Franklin Court, a series of attached and semi-attached homes designed by the firm of Ford, Butler, and Oliver, was brought about by the Garden City Company after Doubleday, Page & Company set up its operations off Franklin Avenue in 1910. Of interest is that Franklin Court sits on a triangular site. Seen here are homes that face inward toward an entrance park, of which Smith approvingly wrote: "[b]y building the two-story stucco, slate-roofed houses close to the encircling roadway, the planners gave each dwelling its own deep, private, walled-in garden, creating a charm and appeal very like that of a Cotswold village in England." (GCVAC.)

GARDEN CITY EAST AERIAL VIEW FACING NORTH, 1949. This is Garden City south of Meadow Street with Franklin Court in the center. The LIRR's branch to Hempstead is at right and the branch that extends toward West Hempstead is at left. The Doubleday Company is at upper left, and Porrier's corner (named after August Porrier, whose small establishment was on the corner of the Doubleday property) lies beneath it. Porrier's accommodated several racing teams that participated in the Vanderbilt Cup meets between 1904 and 1910. The garage where they kept their cars borders on Hempstead and Garden City. The original gardens of Doubleday's Country Life Press facility have been replaced by an additional building and parking lot. The houses moved to Franklin Court when Doubleday was built can be seen at left center on Third Place and Fifth Place. (GCVAC.)

OLIVE FRANCES TJADEN, PROLIFIC ARCHITECT, C. 1945. Brooklyn-born Garden City resident Olive Tjaden (pronounced "jodden," 1904–1997) began her career in 1926, a time when female architects were practically nonexistent. Having opened her office on Seventh Street, among her early creations was the house she and her parents lived in at 104 Eleventh Street (below), done in the style of a French chateau. By 1938, she designed over 200 homes in Garden City, but her fine work was found in many higher-end residential neighborhoods in Nassau County, such as the Five Towns. Tjaden's range of architecture was wide, including religious buildings of varying denominations and commercial architecture, one example being the erstwhile Mack Markowitz Oldsmobile dealership in Hempstead. She would later attribute her success to her ability to discern what women liked to see in their prospective homes. (Both, Olive Tjaden Papers, 15-6-2919 Division of Rare and Manuscript Collections, Cornell University Library.)

LIVE IN AN ATMOSPHERE OF INSPIRING BEAUTY

In the beautiful old town of Garden City, a new community of attractive modern homes has been created by Mott Brothers, offering an opportunity to people of moderate means to live in this ideal community. First class modern schools insure the proper education of children and fine old churches, wide streets and walks lined with shade trees give an air of dignity and grace seldom found elsewhere.

In this ideal environment, Mott Brothers will build for you a home designed to fit your particular needs *at a price you can afford to pay.* Mott Brothers specialize in the design of small homes and no two ever look alike. Prices vary from $6,000 to $15,000. Visit our complete home display today with houses furnished by Frederick Loeser and Company. Open from 11 A. M. to 9 P. M.

MOTT BROTHERS
Garden City

WASHINGTON AVENUE · GARDEN CITY, L. I.

MOTT SECTION ADVERTISEMENT, 1937. In the eastern part of Garden City north of Stewart Avenue is the Mott section, developed during the 1930s by brothers Harold and Edward Mott, well known area builders. This ad points to the advantages that come with living here: "first class modern schools" and "fine old churches," "wide streets," and "walks lined with trees [that] give an air of dignity and grace seldom found elsewhere." That this was during the Great Depression seemed not to matter: this ad was clearly intended for upper-middle-class prospective homebuyers who, the assumption ran, were discerning and responsible people.

GARDEN CITY TOLL LODGE, C. 1935. Elizabeth Ernst, wife of Garden City's toll lodge gatekeeper Christian Ernst, stands with her dog next to the flagpole before the entrance of the Garden City toll lodge at Clinton Road. The toll lodge was one of six designed by John Russell Pope on the length of the now-defunct Long Island Motor Parkway from Hillside Avenue in Queens to Lake Ronkonkoma. As Mildred Smith put it, "Although more suited to the French countryside than to the Hempstead Plains, they added charm to the winding, landscaped motor road." This building was moved to the center of the village in 1989 for use by the chamber of commerce. (GCVAC.)

TOLL LODGE OPERATOR AND HIS DAUGHTER, C. LATE 1920S. The gatekeeper is Christian Ernst, who started his job as the Garden City gatekeeper in 1928. According to Smith, Ernst was proud that he made change for "every famous aviator" who had ever entered or exited the adjacent Roosevelt Field. Standing alongside him is his daughter Emma. (GCVAC.)

GARDEN CITY GARAGE, C. 1920s. After starting out as a storage place for cars used by patrons of the Garden City Hotel, the Garden City Garage was taken over in 1920 by George and Gerald Hughes. Their structure was on the northwest corner of Seventh Street and Franklin Avenue until 1967. The Texas-born brothers enjoyed good reputations for their service to the Garden City community and the quality of their work, as they each applied the mechanical know-how the US Army taught them during World War I. (GCVAC.)

FIRST LT. GERALD HUGHES, 1918. This picture is of Gerald (or "Jerry") Hughes as a reserve military aviator at Hazelhurst Airfield as World War I was drawing to an end. In 1926, Hughes became one of the founders of the Garden City Chamber of Commerce and subsequently its third president. During the 1930s, he was instrumental in getting fellow business leaders to support the creation of 6,000 free municipal parking spaces for customers shopping in Garden City, a novel concept at the time that drew national attention (see page 70). (GCVAC.)

VILLAGE HALL, C. 1930s. Originally the village stables (see page 64), the stately-looking Village Hall at 110 Seventh Street, seen here looking west, was Garden City's first seat of government in its own building. This building was superseded by the present Village Hall on Stewart Avenue that opened in March 1953. (GCVAC.)

BOARD OF TRUSTEES, C. 1925. This group portrait is of the mayor and board of trustees on the second floor of the original Village Hall in the building on Hilton Avenue at Seventh Street. From left to right are (seated) Eugene O'Connor Jr. (police justice), William H. Holden, Lardner V. Morris, Francis B. Hamlin (president), Mayor George L. Hubbell, Campbell T. Hamilton, and George L. Hubbell, Jr., (village counsel); (standing) Eugene R. Courtney and Cornelius R. McKay. (GCVAC.)

HON. GEORGE LORING HUBBELL. Soon after moving to Garden City, George Hubbell (1865–1959) worked hard to further its welfare. He first gained attention as a purchasing agent for the LIRR when he obtained the right of way for a new rail line to run southwest from the village. Foreseeing an influx of visitors who would be impressed by what Garden City had to offer, Hubbell saw to it that the (second) Garden City Hotel would accommodate a greater number of high society guests and their servants. He also had the livery and boarding stables on Seventh Street enlarged and called for more "surreys, runabouts and phaetons" to be made available for general use. In 1897, Hubbell became the general manager of the Garden City Company. He also owned and operated a real estate office on the corner of Seventh Street and what is today Hilton Avenue. Such community standing led to Hubbell's election as Garden City's first president (a post whose title changed to mayor in 1929) after its incorporation in 1919, in which he intermittently served when he was not a trustee until 1932. (GCVAC.)

DEDICATION CEREMONY, MARCH 7, 1953. Here, during the cornerstone laying ceremony of Garden City's new (today's) village hall, Mayor-elect Clinton Corwin hands off a ceremonial trowel in appreciation to the outgoing mayor George R. Murdock. Murdock served from 1943 to 1945, 1950 to 1951, and 1951 to 1953. Corwin's service as trustee and mayor extended over eight years, ending in 1955. (GCVAC.)

FIREHOUSE, C. 1950s. Taken in the 1950s, this photograph facing southeast across Seventh Street shows the original firehouse. The structure is the same as when it was first built in 1912, except that the façade was modified for the two doors for the rigs to pass through. The building's top floor was used for the Village Hall office from 1919 until the stable to its east was converted four years later. This building, along with the old Village Hall, was replaced by commercial buildings in 1953. (GCVAC.)

FIRST POLICE CHIEF, 1922. Featured in this early image are Garden City's first two police chiefs. The first is A.J. Conran (left), and the second is Arthur M. Vanderwater, seen here as a patrolman in front of the police wagon. (GCVAC.)

POLICE FORCE, 1933. Proud members of the local police force stand beside the old Village Hall. From left to right are Officer Lawlor, Officer Blichicki, Officer Davis, Sergeant Vanderwater, Officer Pierce, Officer Berg, Officer Wilson, Officer Bravo, Sergeant Reuter, Officer Wansor, Officer Nesbit, Officer Smith, and Officer Brooks. (GCVAC.)

JOHN W. WYDLER POST OFFICE BUILDING. Built in 1936 as a Depression-era project, this Classical Revival–styled post office was listed in the National Register of Historic Places in 1989. It was designed by Walker & Gillette, consulting architects for the Treasury Department's Office of the Supervising Architect, the federal agency overseeing the design of federal offices from 1852 to 1939. In its lobby is a landmarked painting, *Huckleberry Frolic* by American muralist J. Theodore Johnson. The building was officially renamed in December 1987 for former congressman John W. Wydler, who served from 1963 to 1981.

SECOND GARDEN CITY LIBRARY (FORMER GARDEN CITY COMPANY BUILDING, BEFORE 1958. This lovely building, which superceded the estate office done in by a fire in early 1912, was east of the rail station at Hubbell Plaza. It was razed to make way for the present library, which sits to what would have been its predecessor's left. The former library would have been in the parking lot of the current one.

CORNERSTONE LAYING CEREMONY, JULY 1900. Among the dignitaries welcomed to mark the cornerstone laying for the new county courthouse on the corner of Franklin Avenue and Old Country Road was New York governor and Nassau County's favorite son Theodore Roosevelt. The mood was festive, complete with a band ready to celebrate with song. Mildred Smith cites the *South Side Observer* as having sported a large crayon drawing representing the future courthouse and that a "cornerstone . . . suspended by means of a three-legged derrick above its final resting place at the northeast corner of the building." Nassau County was officially created in 1899. (GCVAC.)

COUNTY COURTHOUSE ON FRANKLIN AVENUE FACING SOUTHWEST, C. 1910S. This is an early and somewhat countrified image of the Nassau County Courthouse. Its administrative wings were added toward the middle of the century. A lone car is riding on Franklin parallel to a trolley at far left. (GCVAC.)

SUFFRAGETTE MARCH, MARCH 1913. Seen here marching alongside the trolley tracks in front of the Nassau County Courthouse is a procession of suffragettes en route to a rally on Front Street in Hempstead. This pageant was organized by "General" Rosalie (Gardiner) Jones, whose honorary title was given her because of her many followers. On the date that this parade took place, an impressive 5,000 people witnessed it along its two-and-a-half-mile route. (GCVAC.)

Junction of the Boulevard and the Old Country Road, Mineola, L. I.

FRANKLIN AVENUE NEAR THE CORNER WITH OLD COUNTRY ROAD, C. 1910s. Looking north from the left-hand side of the street, a woman is walking parallel to the Nassau County Courthouse. In the distance is the northern extremity of Garden City, which bordered the Village of Mineola. The Denton Building, one of Mineola's early commercial buildings, is at back left; to its right is Johren's Hotel. To the left of the hotel is the trolley line's terminus. (GCVAC.)

Three

AFFLUENCE AS A WAY OF LIFE

COLONEL ROOSEVELT AT DOUBLEDAY OPENING, JULY 10, 1910. A smiling Theodore Roosevelt acknowledges the audience on Doubleday Publishing's opening day. Having Roosevelt speak a few words as an honored guest only reinforced Doubleday's importance to the future of the Garden City community. While Garden City's character experienced a major change with Doubleday's presence in the area, it also marked the start of a longstanding trend that had city-based companies move their operations to the open spaces that the then suburbs were known to have. (GCVAC.)

VILLAGE STABLES, 1874. A L'Hommedieu creation, this 130-foot-long structure was on the south side of Seventh Street halfway between Hilton and Franklin Avenues and aptly near the Garden City Hotel. Built in 1872, the stables were intended for patrons of the Garden City hotel—most notably, members of the Meadow Brook Hunt Club who were wont to lodge there—but in time, its utility was extended to the general public. Note the entrance driveway at the center, which ran to a stable yard behind. Along with it were the quarters for coachmen and stable staff near the corner of Franklin Avenue. The building was converted to the Village Hall in 1927 (see page 56). (GCVAC.)

EARLY COMMERCIAL SCENE, C. 1870s. This early scene of Garden City's budding business district on Seventh Street (which, thanks especially to the horse-drawn carriage, resembles something out of a Western) faces northeast across Hilton Avenue on the east side of the street. From this perspective, there are only two sets of modest storefronts, but the types of businesses they housed cannot be determined. Note the lone proprietor of one standing before the doorway. As time progressed, Garden City's business district would blossom. (GCVAC.)

SEVENTH STREET, 1936. This fine aerial view facing northeast is of Seventh Street, at bottom center, and Franklin Avenue, which traverses in a slant at top. Notice the rail line wrapping around as it extends to Mineola at far right, the Garden City Garage's large black roof at center, and the spire of Best & Co. (see page 69) at the corner of Stewart and Franklin Avenues. Of note are the new parking fields, an innovation at the time thanks to Gerald Hughes (see page 70). The Hampshire House apartment building is on Seventh Street and the Franklin Apartments are on the east side of Franklin Avenue. Village Hall is at bottom center; the new Village Hall would be in the treed area at left center. (GCVAC.)

WALTER HINES PAGE, DOUBLEDAY PRESIDENT, c. 1910s. A Garden City resident who lived at 32 Cathedral Avenue who also had a distinguished résumé, Walter Page (1855–1918) was a seasoned journalist who later served in the diplomatic corps, having risen through its ranks to be ambassador to the United Kingdom during World War I. In the Garden City area, he was a partner of Doubleday, Page & Company beginning in 1900. Page's leadership paved the way for Doubleday to grow into a publishing powerhouse. (GCVAC.)

TIMOTHY L. WOODRUFF. Former lieutenant governor Woodruff (1858–1913) was the first person to serve under three consecutive governors, including Theodore Roosevelt, who saw in him a staunch political ally. By the time Woodruff set his sights on Garden City, his business acumen, particularly in Brooklyn waterfront real estate, was well known, as were his political connections. Woodruff entered in partnership with Gage Tarbell (see page 48) when the latter was increasingly immersed in the development of the Garden City Estates; Woodruff was also instrumental in bringing the Doubleday publishing house to Garden City. (GCVAC.)

DOUBLEDAY PUBLISHING COMPANY, SUMMER 1947. In this scene, a large contingent of female employees is exiting the Doubleday Company building off Franklin Avenue. Founded as the Doubleday & McClure Company 50 years earlier and then Doubleday, Page in 1910, in 1927 it merged with the George H. Doran Company to become Doubleday Doran; in 1944, it acquired Blakiston, a Philadelphia-based medical publisher. By the time this photograph was taken in 1947, Doubleday was the largest publishing firm in the United States. (GCVAC.)

LIRR ENGINE 113 AT DOUBLEDAY, 1945. This locomotive's siding ran between Doubleday's main Country Life Press building and annex and was used to unload raw materials, like paper, at the plant to make books. Integral to Doubleday's operations, the engine, which connected to today's defunct West Hempstead branch of the LIRR, also shipped out finished books to Doubleday's distribution sites. (GCVAC.)

COUNTRY LIFE PRESS STATION. Situated behind the Country Life Press building (see page 67), the Country Life Press station, built in 1913 behind the Doubleday plant at Doubleday's request, served the riding public on the Hempstead branch of the LIRR. Its location is close to where the Hempstead Interlocking Tower used to be, or where the Wye parking lot is today. (GCVAC.)

FRANKLIN AVENUE, c. 1930s. In this scene, Franklin Avenue is starting to assume characteristics similar to what it is today: a modern, posh commercial center with parked cars as a fixture.

UPSCALE STORES, C. 1940S. Among the stores that Garden City attracted by the mid-20th century was this pair of upscale retail outlets. Frederick Loeser & Co. (right) was a major department store based in Brooklyn; Best & Co. (below) was one whose flagship store was at one point along the Ladies' Mile in Manhattan. Founded as Loeser and Dinkinspiel in 1860 by Frederick Loeser, a German immigrant, Frederick Loeser & Co. humbly started out as an embroidery and trimmings store, closely resembling Alexander Stewart's mercantile debut. Founded in 1879 by Albert Best, Best & Co. started as a clothing store for children but soon became a commercial force to be reckoned with, competing against the likes of B. Altman's, Gorham's, and even Tiffany's. Best & Co. later branched out across the country, including in Garden City's northern neighbor Manhasset in 1928 before its presence here, facing north on the corner of Stewart and Franklin Avenues. Best & Co. was liquidated in 1970 and Loeser's was replaced by a branch of Abraham and Strauss. (Both, GCVAC.)

PARKING FIELD BEHIND LOESER'S, 1950s. This ordinary scene of a parking field behind Loeser's store filled to capacity was the result of an important initiative undertaken 20 years earlier by Gerald Hughes to have the village install up to 6,000 accessible parking spaces throughout Garden City for shoppers. The chamber of commerce's follow-through on his idea drew national attention, and lent to the view that Garden City was fast becoming a quintessential suburban community. The new Franklin Simon building is at top center. (GCVAC.)

BLOOMINGDALE'S, 1972. Sited on the northeast corner of Franklin Avenue and Eleventh Street, this massive 250,000-square-foot, four-level retail outlet of the famous Bloomingdale's department store was designed by architect Edward Durrell Stone. After some initial reluctance to branch out to the suburbs, Bloomingdale's finally followed the trend set by its predecessors, Frederick Loeser's and Best's, Lord and Taylor's, and Saks Fifth Avenue years before. According to the *New York Times,* when this outlet opened in 1972, it was Bloomingdale's largest branch, with a parking garage that accommodated 1,200 cars. Today, the building is being converted to suit the needs of NYU Langone (Winthrop) Hospital. (GCVAC.)

SAKS GROUND BREAKING, 1960. The arrival of another luxury retail giant, Saks Fifth Avenue, further solidified Garden City's reputation as a high-class shopping district. In this photograph, Saks president Adam Gimbel and Garden City mayor William Maskanka are breaking ground for construction on Franklin Avenue. Behind them smiling is Garden City Chamber of Commerce president Frank Wilson. (GCVAC.)

Poor Man's Car of the Future, 1929. New Haven–based *Illustrated Current News* ran this interesting ad for a compact car called the Martin Dart, the brainchild of airplane manufacturer and Garden City resident James V. Martin. The ad states that the Dart was "a tiny car, unique in construction and remarkable in performance," and "made to sell for $200 and probably to be marketed through mail order distribution." As a further consideration for customers, "[i]t is planned to have it shipped in a weather-proof packing case with a hinged door that can serve as its garage."

Garden City Gun Club, 1907. As one of two area gun clubs (with the other being the Carteret Gun Club, first located in central Garden City on the site of Carteret Place, and later relocated to the eastern outskirts of Garden City, where Eisenhower Park stands today), the Garden City Gun Club hosted clay pigeon shooting. The club was adjacent to nearby golf links, and its membership included many enthusiasts who hailed from the Garden City area. (GCVAC.)

WALTER J. TRAVIS,
Amateur Champion of 1900.

FINDLAY S. DOUGLAS,
Runner-Up.

HERBERT M. HARRIMAN,
Amateur Champion of 1899.

A. G. LOCKWOOD.

HARRIMAN PUTTING.

THE HOME HOLE, GARDEN CITY LINKS.

TRAVIS DRIVING FROM THE FIRST TEE.

LOCKWOOD DRIVING.

EARLY GOLFERS, 1900. Garden City's reputation as a golfing mecca is apparent in this *Harper's Weekly* photograph collage picturing golfers in the National Amateur Golf Championship in July 1900. Among them was Walter J. Travis, who amassed at least 18 amateur tournament titles between 1900 and 1916 (not including nine wins in the Garden City Golf Club's invitational, now the Travis Memorial); Findlay Douglas, who won three amateur tournaments starting in 1898 and went on to become a founding member of the National Golf Links of America and vice president of the US Golf Association; well-known socialite Herbert H. Harriman, winner of the US amateur championship and metropolitan amateur in 1899, the first year it was held; and Boston's Arthur G. Lockwood, whose claim to fame came in September 1903 when he defeated 37 entrants to capture the first Massachusetts amateur title at Myopia Hunt Club.

THE CASINO, 1907. Built as a small inn for visitors of the cathedral, the Casino was initially called the Stewart Arms. Ten years later, it was redesigned by Stanford White, who also drew plans for the Garden City Hotel. Despite its name, this building was never intended to be a gambling house but rather a sophisticated tennis club and meeting place for the social elite, which it still is. Today, the club is alive and well and filled with tradition. (GCVAC.)

GARDEN CITY GOLF CLUB AND LAKE CORNELIA, MID-1907. Facing northeast across the lake (popularly called Hubbell's Pond) lies the Garden City Golf Club, founded in 1899 as the Garden City Men's Club as a way to distinguish it from the other area clubs. (It remains one of the few exclusively men's clubs in the country.) The golf course, first known as the Island Golf Links, was designed by Devereux Emmet and opened two years earlier with only nine holes meant for guests at the Garden City Hotel. It then expanded to 18 holes and covered 6,000 yards in total, making it the longest course in the entire country. Its prestige allowed it to host the US Open in 1902. The lake, named after Cornelia Stewart, first came after workers filled a depression that resulted after sand and gravel were dug for local roads and topsoil for a park designed to surround the first Garden City Hotel. A two-foot layer of clay lined the excavation area, and a dam contains it at the south end.

SALISBURY LINKS, C. 1915. This is the south side of the Salisbury Links clubhouse, built in 1907 at first the public answer to the Garden City Golf Club. It proved so popular that by 1916, it was made private once again and renamed Cherry Valley Golf Club. However, Joseph J. Lannin (see page 41) reversed its status yet again when he bought a large piece of property east of the village and developed what was to be a new incarnation of Salisbury Links in 1918; by the mid-1920s, he constructed a five-course complex pompously called "The Sports Center of America."

GARDEN CITY ESTATES CLUBHOUSE, C. 1920s. As Garden City's development expanded into Garden City Estates, it followed that the latter would have its own clubhouse as well. According to the promotional book *Garden City Estates*, "The Garden City Estates Club House is with enjoyable features, such as are found in most of the metropolitan clubs, and is the scene of frequent social gatherings. The Club, together with its tennis courts and croquet grounds, is conducted for the benefit of the residents and their friends. A competent steward is in charge." It was converted to a private dwelling when the Garden City Country Club opened in 1916. (GCVAC.)

GARDEN CITY COUNTRY CLUB, C. 1940S. Here, a group of player-spectators silently observe one of their own landing a putt on the 18th green on a crisp fall day. This scene is northeast to the side and rear of the clubhouse.

GIL NICHOLS AND WALTER SCHRIEBER, OCTOBER 1939. Posing with an air of calm are Deepdale veteran pro Gil Nichols (left) and former Metropolitan PGA titleholder Walter Schrieber at the Garden City Country Club course, taking part in the Metropolitan PGA Scotch Foursome tournament. They led with a score of 75 for the morning round, but from there things went downhill as their score rose to 84 by afternoon. The match was won by Fresh Meadow's Al Ciuci and Hudson Valley's Alec Watson, who together scored an impressive 150 for 36 holes.

THE 31ST ANNUAL TILT FOR US WOMEN'S GOLF TITLE, OCTOBER 1930. While taken nine years earlier than the prior image, this one shows that the social prestige associated with golf tournaments was not limited to men. This group of contestants at the Cherry Valley Golf Club, from left to right, are New York's own Glenna Collotte, France's Simono Thien de la Chaume, Wisconsin's Bernice Wall, Canada's Ada McKenzie, Oregon's Helen Payson, Pennsylvania's Edith Quier, and California's Virginia Vam Wie.

13TH ANNUAL FATHER AND SON GOLF ASSOCIATION TOURNAMENT, 1938. From the looks of this photograph, there seemed to be no finer way for the fathers and sons in the community's upper echelon to bond than through a friendly rivalry on the links. This scene, which looks north at the putting contest, was taken from the clubhouse. Given the silhouettes of relaxed spectators in comfortable wicker chairs, one senses how sophisticated this setting is. (GCVAC.)

PLAYERS AND SPECTATORS, AUGUST/SEPTEMBER 1938. Here, at the Cherry Valley Golf Club, is a group of smart-looking observers watching the end of the afternoon rounds of the father-son tournament. The Oakland Golf Club's Joseph and Gordon Upton of Great Neck went on to win over last year's champions Perley and Olin Boone, recording 96-30-66 at 6 under par.

WINNERS. One cannot help but see the pride the elder Upton felt for his son Gordon, who is holding their trophy and basking in their shared victory. (The Boones, meanwhile, finished second overall with 92-20-72 at even par.)

HIGH SCHOOL DANCE BY THE POOL. This large get-together shows many young people who are dressed to impress, with some dancing—or at least one who looks like she is encouraging her partner to dance—and another mugging for the camera in front. (GCVAC.)

ICE SKATING ON LAKE CORNELIA, C. 1960s. Ice skaters take a break in a warming shelter alongside Lake Cornelia, also known locally as Hubbell's Pond. Ice skating on Lake Cornelia was a longstanding community tradition, beginning with members of the St. Paul's hockey team more than a century ago. Skating on the lake ended due to its inability to form thick enough ice. (GCVAC.)

ST. JOSEPH'S CHURCH, C. 1910S. Built to suit the growing religious needs of incoming Catholic parishioners to the Garden City area, this is the original St. Joseph's Church with its rectory, facing west from Franklin Avenue. As a recently added trolley line running from Mineola down Franklin Avenue helped with the arrival of additional parishioners, the church's groundbreaking took place in September 1903 and its cornerstone laying two months after that. Its dedication came in May 1905, but the church would be replaced by a newer structure in 1953. (GCVAC.)

GARDEN CITY COMMUNITY CHURCH, c. 1940s. Facing north from Stewart Avenue was the second location of the Garden City Community Church. Once a private home between Whitehall Boulevard and Brompton Road, it then served as a church from 1937 to 1951. As the sign indicates, Rev. John Gardner was minister of the congregation. (GCVAC.)

CHILDREN'S PARADE AND MAY FESTIVAL, 1920. A procession of children on Cathedral Avenue at Seventh Street (above) begins in front of their school, which today is the administration building for the Garden City Union Free School District. They made their way to a day's outing awaiting them in the village park (below) at the northeast corner of Stewart and Rockaway Avenues. The day's festivities were meant to greet the new spring season: note the maypole at the back of the procession. The girl at center below who is gesturing is presumably there to regale her young visitors with a tale of some kind. (Both, GCVAC.)

STRATFORD SCHOOL FRONT ENTRANCE. In this undated but undeniably adorable photograph, two children are soon about to enter the world of wonder awaiting them at the Stratford School. Built in the Estates section just as Garden City was becoming a suburban community, it opened in 1930 to handle the rapidly increasing school population in the west part of the village. Today, it is part of the Garden City School district, serving youngsters in the second to fifth grades. (GCVAC.)

DISMISSAL, STEWART SCHOOL, C. 1960s. The children's glee is apparent as they exit the Stewart School, whose rear is seen here, on their way to cross Clinton Road at Huntington Road. What was racing through their minds on this wintry day: were they happy to leave a tough school day behind? Was the winter break at hand? It may never be known. (GCVAC.)

FORMER GARDEN CITY HIGH SCHOOL. What is today the Cherry Valley Middle School at the southwest corner of Cherry Valley Avenue and Stewart Avenue originally educated primary school students. It then housed secondary school students (with the exception of seventh graders, who were placed in what is currently the school district's administration building across the street). Principal John C. Coulbourn (the school's first) oversaw educators who were tops in their fields: John Warriner (English), John Horton (English), Milton Weiler (fine arts), J. Noel Corbridge (chemistry), Tom Miner (physics), John Orban (science), John Steinberg (social studies), and Frances Jennings (Latin). According to one account, the school was true to the historic character of the area as it "took on many of the characteristics of a prep school." Renowned yachtsman Sir Thomas Lipton honored the community by donating the mast of his *Shamrock IV* for the school's flagpole, seen here, which is how the school yearbook's got its name. (GCVAC.)

GARDEN CITY HIGH SCHOOL, BUILT IN 1955. Facing north to the Long Island Railroad tracks and Mineola at the top, this view of the high school (center) also includes Garden City Estates among the trees to the left, Merillon Avenue diagonally from upper left to lower right and merging with Rockaway Avenue, which sweeps north around the Garden City Golf Club to its right. A large stormwater recharge basin is just south of the tracks. (GCVAC.)

ADELPHI UNIVERSITY, C. 1930. Today, Adelphi is Long Island's oldest private coeducational institution of higher learning. Its roots can be traced to the founding of the Adelphi Academy, a private girls' preparatory school in Brooklyn in 1863. In June 1896, it was incorporated by the state (thanks in no small measure to Lt. Gov. Timothy Woodruff), with Charles Herbert Levermore installed as president. Although coed at first, by 1917, Adelphi was exclusively a women's college, with a curriculum that emphasized teacher education. The need for it to expand had Adelphi move to Garden City, where it opened in 1929. This postcard view faces northeast with the college's three original buildings; from left to right are Levermore Hall, Blodgett Hall, and Woodruff Hall. St. Paul's School is visible in the back, and the scruffy land on which these buildings sit is where the Hempstead Plains is located.

HONORED GUEST SPEAKER, MAY 6, 1944. Thanks to the passage of the Bolton Act, which called for funding the training of nurses enrolled in the US Cadet Nurse Corps in schools such as Adelphi, the university experienced a sharp uptick of registrants by the end of 1943. To accommodate these students on campus, today's Alumnae and Harvey Halls were designated student dorms. At the dedication ceremonies, First Lady Eleanor Roosevelt was invited to say a few words of appreciation, stating, "I am very glad that in a time of war we can dedicate a building which, while it is dedicated to war service now, will continue to be of service to this college and this community after the war is over." To her right is the chairman of the board of directors, James E. Stiles; to her left, gesturing, is university president Paul D. Eddy. Beside Eddy is dean Ruth S. Harley.

AT EASE. In this relaxed scene, two students on the second story balcony of Adelphi's Blodgett Hall are facing out toward the lawn below. This image harkens to Adelphi's infancy when it was a women's academy, only becoming coed during World War II. Blodgett Hall was named after the university's third president, Dr. Frank D. Blodgett, who oversaw Adelphi's transition to Garden City. (GCVAC.)

TEST BLACKOUT WORKERS, OCTOBER 1941. As Pres. Franklin D. Roosevelt grew concerned over the expanding world war, he felt it was important to beef up home defense measures. One was to have communities set up civil defense councils. Here, even though the attack on Pearl Harbor was two months into the future, a local coordination effort at the Mineola courthouse on Franklin Avenue for a metropolitan-wide blackout test is underway. In this busy scene, volunteers are fielding calls. Blackouts were necessary to prevent enemy aircraft from bombing key targets—civilian ones included. (GCVAC.)

TEST BLACKOUT WORKERS, OCTOBER 1941. Civil Defense volunteers are examining locations in Garden City as the test blackout throughout the metropolitan area was taking place. Note how the Garden City area is broken down into various sections; the curved section below the "3" is the Mott area. (GCVAC.)

AMBULANCE SERVICE, CIVIL PROTECTION UNIT, C. 1940S. As part of the Civilian Protection Unit in Garden City, three dedicated, serious-minded ambulance volunteers are on Seventh Street in front of the firehouse. (GCVAC.)

LIFESAVING DRILL, OCTOBER 1941. As part of local civil defense initiatives, the Garden City Fire Department (GCFD) conducted its own drills meant to rescue local citizens in the event of an airborne attack. As this photograph was taken, a 15-minute test blackout took place, and the GCFD responded in kind, with two firefighters giving first aid to two "victims" of an air raid. This is taking place at Eleventh Street and Franklin Avenue.

CIVIL DEFENSE PAPER DRIVE, 1942. Paper was among the rationed materials on the home front during World War II, and so recycling programs were instituted. Here is an enthusiastic group of boys (perhaps Boy Scouts) standing high on a pile of used paper in a dump truck, doing their part to ensure that not a scrap goes to waste. The grown men in front, outwardly appreciative of this drive, may have been officials of the local civil defense team. (GCVAC.)

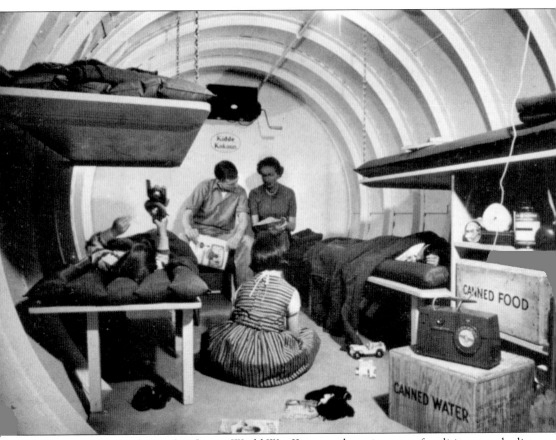

"KIDDE KOKOON," c. 1950s. Just as World War II imposed a unique set of realities onto the lives of ordinary Americans, so did the Cold War soon thereafter. Here, quite staged, is a local family in an underground bomb shelter fancifully named "Kidde Kokoon," manufactured by Walter Kidde Nuclear Laboratories on Stewart Avenue east of Garden City. Despite the dire circumstances that would have brought this family into this shelter to begin with, this image takes pains to show that, come what may, life for the American people would proceed as normally as possible. (GCVAC.)

Four

CALL OF DUTY

THE 165TH INFANTRY'S ARRIVAL TO CAMP MILLS, AUGUST 1917. On August 20, 1917, the 165th Infantry Regiment, New York National Guard, arrived at Camp Mills (named after Maj. Gen. Albert Mills, superintendent of West Point). The 165th was integral to the 42nd Rainbow Division, having fought the enemy during St. Mihilel in September and then Meuse-Argonne in October, as part of the American Expeditionary Force's 100-day offensive that helped bring an end to World War I. (GCVAC.)

CAMP MILLS ENTRANCE, 1917. In this scene facing west across Clinton Road to the Clinton Road train station, a group is awaiting the troops marching from the Hempstead Crossing railroad station and Stewart Avenue, down Clinton Road and past this point to Camp Mills, north of the tracks to the left. A freight car stands on one side off the tracks, while a trolley car from the Garden City station is on the other. A Western Union telegraph sign is mounted to the pole in front of the station. (GCVAC.)

CAMP SCENE, 1917. In this postcard scene, there is much activity on what appears to be a fine day (some onlookers are in their undershirts). Perhaps the marching soldiers in front are recent arrivals to Camp Mills, but since it was an embarkation camp at first, it is also just as likely that these men received their marching orders and are being shipped out. Notice the propped-up tents in back; their sturdy appearance was only temporary in the late autumn's colder and more inclement weather, much to the dismay of camp leaders. (GCVAC.)

WELL-ORDERED CAMPGROUND, 1917. Taken from a southeastern perspective, this sweeping view shows the tent encampment at Camp Mills abutting the rail line parallel to Clinton Road (the original Stewart Line). The wagon train in front was perhaps used to transport bulk items from the station to parts of the camp. As far as the eye can see are rows of canvas tents that sheltered the enlisted men. Officers made do with tents also, but they were individualized. A ruinous winter storm that came within a few months after this photograph was taken necessitated the construction of sturdier barracks (see page 100). (GCVAC.)

MORNING ROUTINE, 1917. In this candid photograph, bare-chested soldiers are up for their morning wash (note some holding towels), which took some doing in Camp Mills's early days due to its lack of permanent facilities. In December 1917, the *Brooklyn Eagle* observed, "There was no bathhouse and the only means of taking a bath was to heat a bucket of water and take a sponge bath in one's tent or wait until one could get a pass and go into town to a public bathhouse." At center is a soldier with his mouth open before a commanding officer, possibly to see what, if anything, could have ailed him.

CHOW LINE, 1917. A long line of soldiers are waiting for their breakfast in a photograph that shows camp life at its earthiest. Many are clad in just their undershirts, which could mean that they just finished their morning exercises, whether calisthenics or military drills. (GCVAC.)

94

CHOPPING WOOD. One mundane yet important task assigned to soldiers was chopping wood, necessary to light fires to cook food and to provide warmth as the weather grew colder and harsher. Soldiers risked being reprimanded if they did not chop their wood allotment.

DIAMOND HITCH, MAY 20, 1918. In this postcard scene, soldiers observe how to load a pack-saddle on a horse using a lashing technique known as a diamond hitch. Given that every muscle of a pack animal's body moves when it is in motion, the diamond hitch would help secure pack bags, pack boxes, or similar gear onto the saddle the animal was wearing.

B-3 Camp Mills, 1917—After a Drill

AFTER A DRILL, 1917. After a set of strenuous exercises, which could have included unfurling the tents seen here in case a real need to do so ever arose, soldiers were eager to have even a momentary respite. Here, a group of them are posing affably for the photographer.

We are having jolly good times now in *like H—ll*

CAMP MILLS

"CAMPY" POSTCARD. This playful postcard was meant to put the recipient's mind at ease about what life for the sender was like at Camp Mills (but given the sender's remark at upper right, he was nobody's fool). In the beginning, camp conditions made life a distinct challenge for the enlisted men, especially during the winter. Things later got so bad that there were calls to close the camp altogether. By 1918, Camp Mills was refurbished, with soldier barracks and other permanent structures erected.

The 42nd Division in Review (1917). Here, the 42nd Division is under review before Maj. Gen. William A. Mann and his staff. Mann (1854–1934) earned distinction as the commander of the 17th Infantry Brigade during the Spanish American War, having participated in the battle of El Caney, where he received the Silver Star, and in the Siege of Santiago. Seen here in formation, the soldiers are reminiscent of the well-disciplined cadets who stood before St. Paul's school (see page 33). (GCVAC.)

CHOWING DOWN. During Camp Mills's first year of operations in 1917, soldiers who finished their morning drills took their midday meal while seated on the ground, much like Boy Scouts on a campout. Naturally, this state of affairs could continue for only so long, given the men's growing discomfiture. But their love of country had them stick it out. This image is from a postcard titled "Free and Easy Lunch."

VISITORS DAY, 1917. One of the ways to lift troop morale was to have visitors come and spend some quality time with their on-site significant others. Although historian Richard Welch believes this image was staged for the purpose of this postcard, it nevertheless conveys how meaningful such visits were to those in camp.

"OUT TO TRIM THE KAISER." Internally, Camp Mills was forced to contend with the bigotry that some units showed toward others, the origins of which were traceable to that of their forebearers during the Civil War. Still, the common foe they all faced required unconditional unity among the ranks. With their chalk message and cartoons, these soldiers fully understood that their overriding mission was to ensure that the Kaiser (the Central Powers) had to be "trimmed," meaning defeated. "Bill" was a waggish reference to Germany's Kaiser Wilhelm II. (GCVAC.)

FIRE! As if dealing with the camp's substandard conditions was not enough, a grass fire broke out on the grounds in 1917 near the tents of the 3rd Foreign Detachment of the Signal Corps, which was close to the camp's aviation field. To contain the fire, the camp's military police and detachments coordinated with volunteer fire departments from the communities of Hempstead and Westbury. Despite this frightening scene, neither tents, equipment, or anything of consequence were severely affected. When the camp was restructured the following year, fire stations were set up to deal with potential issues.

DISASTER, 1917 OR EARLY 1918. A newspaper called this scene "a total wreck" after the season's first winter storm barreled through the camp, damaging already vulnerable tents. (The soldiers who did not ship overseas yet had to relocate, as the *New York Times* put it, "to one of the southern camps.") Surveying the damage are individuals from the Quartermaster's Corps.

NEW YORK STREET ENTRANCE, 1918. This entrance was one block north of the main entrance on Clinton Road. After the weather-related mishaps it experienced in 1917, Camp Mills got a makeover thanks to funding from the War Department. As part of the reconstruction effort, the Garden City Water Company built a water system so running water could be brought to the camp. Much to the soldiers' satisfaction, sturdy barracks such as those seen here were also built. The guard at the intersection is ostensibly guiding traffic along a newly paved roadway.

LANDSCAPING, 1918. The federal government's revitalization of Camp Mills brought needed order to the place. The camp's appearance improved drastically thanks to Garden City resident Francis B. Clarke overseeing much of the landscaping. Here, the fruit of her efforts is on full display. (GCVAC.)

INSPECTION AND REVIEW OF THE RAINBOW DIVISION (42ND)
By Secretary of War Newton D. Baker – CAMP MILLS – Sept 1917 –
SOON TO LEAVE FOR THE FRONT
— IN FRANCE —
Copyright
Stafford Meeson
BALDWIN N.Y.

RAINBOW DIVISION IN REVIEW, SEPTEMBER 1917. Somewhere in this image by Stafford Meeson, a photographer from nearby Baldwin, is Secretary of War Newton D. Baker reviewing the 42nd Rainbow Division days before it left for combat in France. Under the leadership of Gen. William A. Mann, the 42nd was comprise of National Guard units from 26 states and the District of Columbia. In the summer of 1917, the 42nd was activated after America's entry into the war, as one of the divisions of the American Expeditionary Force. One proud regiment was the 165th (see page 91). The spectators who lined the procession likely viewed the parade with a flush of pride, but also with an air of solemnity the moment called for. (GCVAC.)

ON TO CAMP MILLS, DECEMBER 1918. In this telling scene at Long Island City (LIC), the first troops who fought overseas will soon make their way home via ferry from LIC to Camp Mills, where they will be processed and eventually discharged from service. Here, along with the photographer, a throng of well-wishers is greeting and cheering our doughboys as they debarked from their transport ship, the *Mauretania*.

CAMP OFFICERS, 1918. Col. Richard Pickering, Camp Mills's commanding officer, and his staff who helped him administer the needs of the camp are pictured here. From left to right are (seated) liaison officer John Hemus, ? Edwards, ? Darling, Pickering, ? Kimball, ? quartermaster Smith, ? Tuckerman, and ? Haupt; (standing) ? Roddy, ? Harris, ? Darrow, ? Edmondson, Lt. Col. Busch, and ? Crosby. (GCVAC.)

NURSES GROUP, 1918. The work by Camp Mills's dedicated nursing staff was particularly vital for soldiers arriving from overseas. And yet they were soon overwhelmed; according to author James McKenna, "By mid-October [1918], Camp Mills was quarantined as the number of Spanish influenza patients jumped from a little over 47 cases in September to more than 1,100 cases by October 10, with an average of 130 new cases reported daily." Soldiers were first treated at the Mineola Fairgrounds in Garden City before a 2,500-bed base hospital was built on Transverse Road. (GCVAC.)

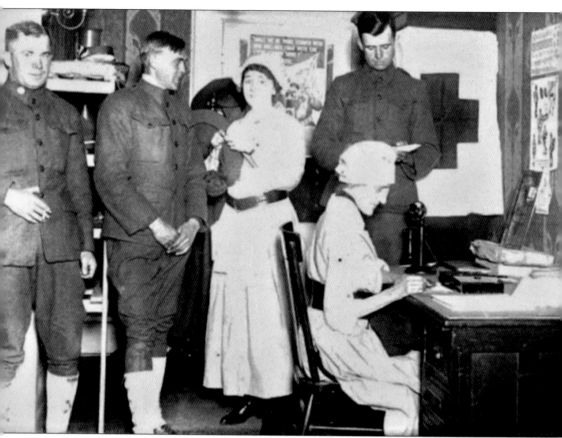

SOLDIERS AND RED CROSS NURSES, SEPTEMBER 1917. Friendly and obliging, two Red Cross nurses are being of service to some soldiers, whether it was repairing an article of clothing (center) or finishing necessary paperwork for them to be discharged from the hospital with a clean bill of health. (GCVAC.)

BASE HOSPITAL, MARCH 13, 1919. Built in 1918 to replace the temporary facility at the Mineola Fairgrounds, Camp Mills's impressive base hospital contained 2,500 beds. It was separate from Camp Mills itself, on a half-mile area east of Washington Avenue. The road is present-day Transverse Road. This rare photograph, taken from where the nurses were stationed, faces southwest and shows that trees were not neglected in the rush to construct the facility. The whole complex was removed by the early 1920s. Notice the chimney of the power plant in the background, which replaced the steam locomotive that was brought in to provide heat for the complex. (GCVAC.)

AMBULANCE CORPS. By 1918, a modernized ambulance corps was put into service to transport ailing soldiers to the camp hospital for treatment. Once the Spanish flu pandemic of 1918 made itself felt in the camp, the corps played a vital role in transporting afflicted soldiers to the Mineola Fairgrounds to the camp's north, a more isolated location, to quarantine them.

CLEAN KITCHEN. Part of Camp Mills's restoration is apparent in this postcard view of a clean and sanitary hospital kitchen where a nurse or aide is in the middle of preparing something. The threat of the Spanish flu necessitated preventive measures, the foremost being clean and orderly hospital conditions.

RECUPERATION. As soldiers convalesced and were deemed well enough to briefly leave their hospital beds, they congregated in meeting areas at the Red Cross building, such as in this scene, where they engaged in some reading or playing cards or dominoes, all as Red Cross nurses assisted them and joined in their camaraderie.

NATIONAL CATHOLIC WAR COUNCIL, 1918. This elegant structure on the east side of Clinton Road, just north of Poplar Street, housed the local chapter of the National Catholic War Council. Inspired by the call for Prohibition and the threat of federalization of education, the NCWC departments nationwide (consisting of education, legislation, social action, lay organizations, and press and publicity), headed by bishops, gave lay Catholics a voice in current issues, including the Catholic Church's position on the war and related matters. (GCVAC.)

JEWISH WELFARE BOARD. Formed by prominent Jewish Americans in April 1917 as a response to the United States' entry in World War I, the Jewish Welfare Board accommodated the spiritual and material needs of Jewish American soldiers, their families, and even those outside their community, as the bold welcome sign attests. The welfare board organized various war work components throughout the armed forces, at home and overseas, and established a network of agencies that provided key services for its charges, the distribution of non-perishable Kosher foods being but one. This network was designed to complement services offered by the federal government.

JUST GOT BACK, 1919. One minor but touching bit of assistance the Jewish Welfare Board offered were humble postcards like this one that soldiers sent their friends and loved ones to inform them of their arrival at a certain camp. Imagine the utter joy the receiver of this postcard had once they got the news.

HOSTESS HOUSE. Situated on Clinton Road opposite Locust Street near the main entrance of Camp Mills, the YWCA Hostess House (one of many across the country) opened in September 1918 to billet visiting parents, wives, and children of those stationed in the camp. Like a hotel, it rented out rooms for both men and women for overnight stays or for longer durations and had sitting rooms for guests to congregate.

SALVATION ARMY HOTEL, 1918.
At the present-day location of
the Stewart School was the
Salvation Army Hotel, pictured
here before it was later moved
in two sections to neighboring
Hempstead in 1928. While the
Salvation Army's mission was
recognized before World War I, it
first brought its services to Camp
Mills and its vicinity at that time.
Its reputation for social and relief
work was greatly enhanced, as
Gen. Evangeline Booth offered
the organization's services to
Pres. Woodrow Wilson. During
one event in 1917, more than 250
Salvation Army volunteers went
to France to provide soldiers with
needed supplies and baked goods,
including doughnuts. (GCVAC.)

FOR HISTORY'S SAKE, 1919.
Apparently, this solitary soldier
felt Britain's R34 dirigible's
dramatic landing (see page
144) was momentous enough
to have this photograph
taken for posterity.

CANTEEN, 1918. On the south side of Meadow Street, just east of the railroad, was the camp's canteen, or cafeteria (also referred to as the chow hall). Two men from neighboring Mitchel Field have arrived to get a bite to eat: George Burns standing on the porch and ? Hughes crouching in the bushes. The canteen's captain, Esther McDonald, poses with them. (GCVAC.)

MARCHING BAND AND ENLISTED MEN'S DANCE, 1918. If recognized by their superiors, soldiers who were musically proficient were given a coveted place in the camp's marching band. Band music was essential not only for public shows of patriotism, but for functions on camp grounds such as enlisted men's dances held at the camp's recreation hall (below) on the south side of Recreation Street.

ENLISTED MENS DANCE
RECREATION HALL
CAMP MILLS, N.Y.

GARDEN CITY WAR HERO 1ST LT. WILLIAM BRADFORD TURNER, C. 1918. Sadly, not all soldiers who served overseas were fortunate enough to return to Camp Mills. One of them happened to be Garden City resident (and student of St. Paul's) 1st Lt. William Bradford Turner of the 105th Infantry Regiment, who was killed near Ronssoy, France, on September 27, 1918. For his gallantry and courage in the face of the enemy, Turner received the Medal of Honor. His citation reads:

He led a small group of men to the attack, under terrific artillery and machinegun fire, after they had become separated from the rest of the company in the darkness. Single-handed he rushed an enemy machinegun which had suddenly opened fire on his group and killed the crew with his pistol. He then pressed forward to another machinegun post twenty-five yards away and had killed one gunner himself by the time the remainder of his detachment arrived and put the gun out of action. With the utmost bravery he continued to lead his men over three lines of hostile trenches, cleaning up each one as they advanced, regardless of the fact that he had been wounded three times, and killed several of the enemy in hand-to-hand encounters. After his pistol ammunition was exhausted, this gallant officer seized the rifle of a dead soldier, bayoneted several members of a machinegun crew, and shot the other. Upon reaching the fourth line trench, which was his objective, Lieutenant Turner captured it with the nine men remaining in his group and resisted a hostile counterattack until he was finally surrounded and killed.

Bradford was buried in France's Somme American Cemetery. (GCVAC.)

Five

IN DEFENSE OF COUNTRY

DAWN PATROL, C. 1940s. Sold in a pack of 12 postcards featuring military life at Mitchel Field was this image of soldiers reporting to their daily run at the crack of dawn. Their parachutes figure prominently, as do their headphones. This photograph, along with those on the companion postcards (which, at two by three inches, were all smaller than traditional ones), were all taken by the talented William Hoff, official photographer of LaGuardia Airport.

IN THE DISTANCE. A plane is flying over Aviation Field No. 2, an airfield in the eastern portion of Camp Mills, seen here with tents in the foreground, before the barracks were built in 1918. Mitchel Field later acquired the territory east of the Garden City boundary to expand its aviation operations.

"BOY MAYOR" JOHN PURROY MITCHEL, JUNE 1918. The youngest mayor in New York City history, John Purroy Mitchel (1879–1918) made his name as the leader of a municipal reform group whose intent was to wrestle municipal government from the power of Tammany Hall. He successfully ran for mayor on the Fusion Party ticket, and his administration won praise for its efficiency, reform measures (especially in the police department), and duty to the people. But his popularity started to wane thanks to his unpopular policies over the city's finances and education. After losing his reelection bid, he joined the Air Service, where he eventually achieved the rank of major. But as Mitchel was returning from a short training flight, his plane made an unexpected nosedive. Because he was not fastened in, Mitchel was thrown from the plane and fell 500 feet to his death. This photograph was taken one month earlier. Mitchel Field was named in his honor.

MITCHEL FIELD, APRIL 1928. In this dramatic aerial view is a crowd getting ready to greet the historic arrival of a Junkers W33 monoplane manned by the Bremen Flyers: German aviators Baron Gunther von Huenefeld and Capt. Hermann Koehl, along with their co-pilot Commander James C. Fitzmaurice. Their flight constituted the first east-west transatlantic crossing ever recorded. Flying for 37 hours, they left Baldonnel, Ireland, and eventually landed at Greely Island, Labrador. But their plane suffered damage upon landing, delaying their arrival to New York. Despite this, the three were hailed as heroes, with Pres. Calvin Coolidge awarding them medals, and the City of New York honoring them with a ticker-tape parade.

IC-4 that made the transatlantic voyage in which B.Com. Read was named the new "Columbus of the air"

CURTISS NC-4 FLYING BOAT, 1919. An early giant of a plane designed jointly by the US Navy and a team led by Glenn Curtiss (see page 141), the NC-4 made history as the first American aircraft to fly across the Atlantic. In May 1919, the NC-4 took 19 days (accounting for the five stops it made en route) to make its way from New York to Lisbon, Portugal. As impressive a feat as this was, its significance was overshadowed two weeks later upon news of the first nonstop transatlantic flight by two Royal Air Force pilots, and even more by Charles Lindbergh's momentous flight in 1927. (GCVAC.)

JIMMY WALKER AT MITCHEL FIELD, APRIL 1929. Among the throng of people to receive the incoming Bremen flyers at Mitchel Field was New York mayor Jimmy Walker (center, fedora in hand). Apparently, he made an observation that his assistant Charles Kerrigan (to his left), Capt. W. Bender of Mitchel Field, and Grover Whelan of the New York Reception Committee all found amusing.

MITCHEL FIELD COMPLEX, NOVEMBER 1931. This aerial view is of the sprawling Mitchel Field in the process of being upgraded and modernized. Additions to the base included a newly-built operations building made of brick, and officer domiciles situated along the railroad on the north and east sides of the complex. New hangars for the base had yet to be built, however, as the exposed biplanes at lower right indicate.

INTERIOR, CURTISS-WRIGHT ENGINEERING CORPORATION, 1919. Situated between the LIRR and Stewart Avenue east of Clinton Road was the Curtiss Engineering Corporation, whose production floor is seen here facing east. To the left is a twin-engine Eagle, with its twin landing wheels, the only twin-engine Eagle ever made, as others were either one- or three-engine models. Note the JN-4 "Jenny" fuselage beside it. To the right is a type-F pusher engine flying boat. (GCVAC.)

PULITZER TROPHY RACE, OCTOBER 1925. Posing here are the pilot contestants of an air meet for military aircraft that took place as a leg of the National Air Races at Mitchel Field. Sponsored by the publisher Ralph Pulitzer, this meet was part of a series of pylon and cross-country races held around the country and meant to highlight the scientific advancements aviation could bring. In time, these air meets became prestigious enough to attract prominent names like James Doolittle and Wiley Post. From left to right are Maj. Herbert A. Dargue, Lt. Earl S. Hoag, Lieutenant Bailey, Lieutenant Straham, Lieutenant Ackincad, Lieutenant McCoy, Lieutenant Chanley, Lieutenant McReynolds, Lt. Martinus Stenseth, Lt. R.H. Clark, Lieutenant Gaines, and Lieutenant Heckhurst.

PULITZER TROPHY AIR RACE IN ACTION, OCTOBER 1925. This candid photograph captures the Pulitzer race in progress over Mitchel Field. The sight and sound of so many planes at close range transfixes the spectators below. An officer is observing the planes in flight and, to his left, a photographer is poised to mark the occasion with his tripod camera. (GCVAC.)

O 802.1-876F-8)(7-30-36-10:30A)(12-300) HDQRS, MITCHEL F'LD, N.Y.

MITCHEL FIELD POST HEADQUARTERS, JULY 30, 1936. Seen at the heart of this picture is Mitchel Field's Base Operations Building before a control tower was built on its roof. Today, it is the Student Union at Nassau Community College (NCC). To the left is Building 105, the first Air Force headquarters (today's NCC's Nassau Hall), and behind that is building 104, one of two buildings identified as the Continental Air Command headquarters (today's NCC's V Building). In the background is Mitchel Field's base post exchange (the NCC bookstore).

GATHERING DATA, C. 1930s. Seen here are two soldiers on the roof of Mitchel Field's headquarters, which also served as a weather observation post. One of the soldiers is releasing a wind balloon to record wind direction and velocity for long-range weather forecasting. The instrument between them is a theodolite, a telescopic device that measures angles by gauging the drift of the balloon. The radio mast at center was meant for receiving meteorological reports. Beside it is a rainfall gauge. At the right is a shelter to house other instruments.

RADIO ROOM, MAY 1938. This radio control room in the general headquarters building was where the base commander's latest orders were relayed to airborne pilots. Needless to say, swift and sure communication to pilots was deemed vital so they could execute operations as intended.

Parachute Stunt, July 1929. Landing in Roosevelt Field is parachutist Doc Taylor, who set out to show the effectiveness of a device controlled by a pilot meant to release passengers through a plane's floor. Should there have been a problem in midair, the parachute would still open thanks to an attachment that would automatically estimate the distance necessary for clearance.

"The Life of a Parachute Jumper," February 1932. In this stunning photograph, two parachutists swirling sideways are testing a new kind of parachute, triangular in shape. It was theorized that triangular parachutes would eliminate the unwanted oscillation that slowed a parachutist's descent, which was an unavoidable characteristic of round parachutes.

"War Eagles Lay Their Eggs," 1938. This was the caption for this image as written by the Ohio-based Central Press Association for this sobering image that illustrates the United States' emerging military dominance in the air. Shown is a group of B-10s of the 19th Bombardment Squadron as they dropped a salvo of 600-pound bombs as part of air maneuvers intended to defend the northeast coastline in the event of an attack during the war. The bombers were based at Mitchel Field.

WARDING OFF AERIAL INVADERS, JUNE 1937. War was still in the future when this dramatic photograph was taken, but the nation's defense capabilities were taken seriously regardless. Pictured are anti-aircraft guns of the 62nd Coast Artillery punctuating the night sky during a mock aerial attack on New York City by pursuit planes from Mitchel Field. This exercise was part of Governor Island's tercentenary celebration held on June 19.

MITCHEL FIELD AS EXPERIMENTAL LAB, APRIL 1941. As the country was preparing for the possibility of war, the General Headquarters Air Force planned for a standardized air defense system so the nation's aviation forces could defend any threatened area. The Air Defense Command at Mitchel Field would help standardize equipment, tactics, and procedures. Seen here are anti-aircraft guns and their crews on alert for an expected mock air attack.

DEPLOYED CAMP UPTON TROOPS ARRIVE AT MITCHEL FIELD, DECEMBER 1941. Two days after the attack on Pearl Harbor, steel-helmeted soldiers from eastern Long Island's Camp Upton have made their way to guard the Army airfield after the Atlantic coast received an air-raid warning. By this time, Mitchel Field served as a base for interceptor planes.

Combat Readiness, c. 1930s–1940s. While Mitchel Field's foremost purpose was to train technicians for skills needed for air squad work, they were still soldiers who were required to be combat-ready. In this scene, the men are in the midst of a drill that called on them to use their bayonets, with their captain, Clifford W. Vedder (center), looking on.

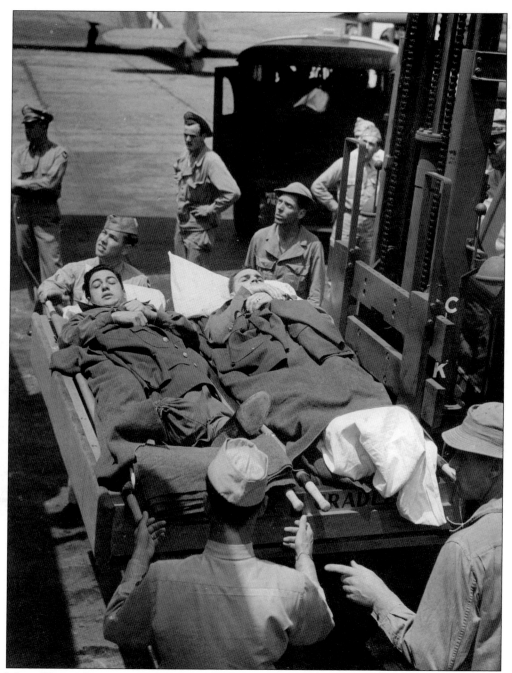

MOCK TRIAGE EXERCISE, 1940s. In addition to drills meant to instill combat readiness among the soldiers were others that focused on treating the wounded. Here, two Army Air Corps men are being lifted into a transport plane that would take them to an appropriate medical facility. At right looking upward is the officer overseeing the operation, Lt. Vernon D. Gibson.

GENERALS COORDINATING, APRIL 1941. In this publicity image, Lt. Gen. Delos C. Emmons points out the four air sectors to the first Air Corps chief in charge of the northeast sector, Maj. Gen. James E. Chaney, as Lt. Col. Arthur I. Ennis holds a map. Emmons was planning a demonstration of the first civilian air-raid spotter system, stating that the United States would employ a nationwide network of more than a half-million civilian spotters, a greater number than those set up in Great Britain.

SERVICING A BOMBER, C. 1940S. In another well-executed photograph, William Hoff captures two servicemen meticulously servicing what appears to be a Douglas B-18 Bolo, a medium-range bomber, which by 1942 was used primarily for training purposes although it would play a role in transport duty and antisubmarine warfare. A B-18 was among the first American aircraft to sink a German U-boat in the Caribbean.

MITCHEL FIELD HANGAR LINE, C. 1940S. In this postcard image, the hangars at Mitchel Field are evident as what appears to be a group of C-47 transport and troop carrier planes taxi on the runway. The C-47 was used extensively throughout the war and remained in operation into the next decade. The hangars to the left have since been torn down, the site now being the location of buildings associated with Nassau Community College.

PACKING A CHUTE, c. 1940s. One cannot overstate the importance of having parachutes in good working order before Air Army Corps personnel don them on their backs. Here, airmen are concentrating on the task of parachute folding, and they appear to take it very seriously.

JAMES H. "JIMMY" DOOLITTLE. Seen here standing before a plane at Mitchel Field years before he led his historic raid on Tokyo during World War II is Jimmy Doolittle (1896–1993). In 1929, Doolittle won acclaim for maneuvering a plane from start to finish using its instruments alone (known as "blind flying"). After achieving this, he returned to Mitchel Field, where he developed the artificial horizon and directional gyroscope, an instrument essential for flight in fog or other inclement weather. (GCVAC.)

STANDING IN FOR HER DAD, 1946. Smiling three-year-old Sharon Vance is receiving the Medal of Honor on behalf of her late father, Col. Leon R. Vance Jr. After having entered into service in Garden City, Vance led the 489th Bombardment Group on a diversionary attack against German coastal defenses off of France as part of D-Day. Despite suffering a near-severed foot, Vance assisted his co-pilot to bring his plane to safety, but then tried a water landing, which the aircraft was not designed to do. The plane landed severely damaged, and an explosion blew Vance clear from the wreckage. After convalescing in the United Kingdom, Vance was en route back to the United States when his C-54 crashed in July 1944, presumably between Iceland and Newfoundland. Although he was to be awarded the Medal of Honor the following January, his widow, Georgette, requested that it be delayed so their daughter could receive it. The Army obliged, and in October 1946, Maj. Gen. James P. Hodges (right) did the honors at Enid Air Force in Oklahoma, later renamed Vance Air Force Base. (GCVAC.)

NURSES AND WACS MARCHING IN REVIEW, C. 1945. Female members of the Women's Army Corps. at Mitchel Field are showing their allegiance to the country, putting their patriotism on full display as they are reviewed by base commander Col. Lewis R. Parker and his staff. (GCVAC.)

MILITARY PARADE, C. 1950s. During the 1950s, there was a growing sense that Mitchel Field was nearing the end of its utility. Flight activity continued at a reduced rate as the Air Defense Command's headquarters now sought a more centralized and protected command center, eventually settling at Ent Air Force Base in Colorado. By 1961, after more than four decades of service, Mitchel Field was decommissioned, its unit reassigned to McGuire Air Force Base in New Jersey; the base formally closed two months later. Seen here is one of the last military parades held on its grounds.

EARLY JET, C. 1950s. Developed by Lockheed Corporation as an all-weather day/night interceptor, by 1950, the F-94 Starfire became part of the first generation of jet aircraft employed by the US Air Force's Air Defense Command. The F-94 is noteworthy because it was the first operational Air Force fighter equipped with an afterburner, which helped in its thrust capability. It was also the first jet-powered all-weather fighter to enter combat, during the Korean War in 1953.

ANOTHER SPEED RECORD, JUST LIKE DAYS OF OLD, JANUARY 1954. As his wife and daughter rush to greet him, Col. Willard W. Millikan is living in the moment in his F-86 Sabre *Minuteman* at Mitchel Field after setting a transcontinental speed record for his flight from Los Angeles. He reached Mitchel Field in four hours, eight minutes, and five seconds, breaking the existing record by five minutes. The Air National Guard assessed that he averaged 615 miles per hour. Produced by North American Aviation, the F-86 was the United States' first swept-wing fighter, which countered the Soviet MIG-15 in dogfights during the Korean War. It is historically significant in that it fought the earliest jet-to-jet battles in American history.

Six

THE HORIZON BECKONED

THRILLED BEYOND HER YEARS, 1931. This plucky sky climber is 19-year-old Elinor Smith (1911–2010), who just landed at Roosevelt Field after a record ascent of 32,500 feet, breaking the previous altitude record of 28,743 feet by Ruth Nichols of Rye, New York. Smith was the youngest person ever to earn a pilot's license from the Fédération Aéronautique Internationale (signed by none other than Orville Wright himself). She went on to break aviation records of all kinds, including being the first pilot to fly under all four of New York City's East River bridges (see page 147), which she did on a bet. Looking back on her life, Smith mused: "To some young women with dreams of a wider world, there seemed to be two paths to follow; one led to Hollywood, the other to a career in the sky. For me there was only one path: I knew from the age of six that I wanted to fly."

BREATHTAKING, 1910. This lovely shot is of grandstand spectators at Washington Avenue Field, also known as Mineola Airfield, in awe of an early airplane overhead. On Glenn Curtiss's recommendation, probably impressed with the flatness of the land, Washington Avenue Field was leased from the Garden City Company by members of the New York Aeronautical Society. Curtiss himself once circled Washington Avenue Field in his famous *Golden Flyer*, also known as *Gold Bug*, for a total of 16 miles in 52 minutes, winning a $10,000 prize sponsored by *Scientific American*. The airfield, during it brief existence between 1909 and 1912, was on the east side of Washington Avenue, south of Old Country Road to Osborne Road. After 1912, its operations were moved to the Hempstead Plains airfield east of Clinton Road. (GCVAC.)

HEMPSTEAD PLAINS AVIATION FIELD

Adjoining Motor Parkway AT CLINTON ROAD **GARDEN CITY, Long Island, N.Y.**

AERO CLUB OF AMERICA'S OFFICIAL FIELD

—— WEEK END AERIAL MEETS ——
Held Under the Auspices of the Week End Meets Association

RACES PROGRAM EVENTS—Prize Point Contests
Military Biplanes vs Scouting Monoplanes

Couriers of the Air in Bomb and Manifesto Dropping Tests

Saturdays and Holidays—3 p.m. 'til Sunset

Saturday and Holiday **ADMISSION 50c.** Parking for Automobiles No Charge for Accomodation

Passenger Flights Booked at Field Daily and Sunday.   Telephone, 1312 Garden City

SUNDAY—Passenger Flying Day   Short Flights $12.50
No Charge for Admission to Field Sunday

Sloane Monoplane "Scout"

Driven by J. Guy Gilpatrick. Competing in these Week End Contests.
SLOANE AEROPLANE CO., 1737 BROADWAY, NEW YORK.   HEMPSTEAD PLAINS AVIATION FIELD D. S. HOUGHTON, Gen'l Mgr. GARDEN CITY, L. I.

☛ MEETS, SEPT. 5, 7, 12, 19, 26.   OCT. 3, 10, 12, 17, 24, 31.

HANDBILL, AERO CLUB OF AMERICA, C. 1910S. In this rare handbill, the Aero Club of America advertises a 10-day aerial meet at the Hempstead Plains Aviation Field. All sorts of program events were planned, including air races and prize contests. Military biplanes were slated to be on display, as were scouting monoplanes and air couriers. Note that the event featured bomb and manifesto dropping tests, all to showcase the latest innovations in aviation and the potential for airmail service. (JDA.)

HEMPSTEAD PLAINS HANGAR AREA, C. 1913. Shown here are early hangars at the Hempstead Plains Airfield, possibly part of Moisant Aviation Training School. The school was founded by Alfred Moisant, brother of famed aviation pioneer John Bevins Moisant, head of the renowned flying circus Moisant International Aviators. The school boasted six Bleriot monoplanes (one being visible in the hangar at left) with 50-horsepower Gnome motors. Among those who trained there was Harriet Quimby (see page 140). (COAM.)

EARLY BIRD MATILDE MOISANT. Moisant (1878–1964) first learned to fly at Hempstead's Moisant Aviation School founded by her brother Alfred, yet named after her husband who died in an air crash. She is on record as being the second female pilot licensed to fly in the United States; this after earning her license after only 32 minutes of in-flight instruction, a record that will likely stand for all time. She also holds the distinction of being the first woman to win an altitude prize, achieving records of 1,200 feet, 1,500 feet, and 3,000 feet. Later, she was the first pilot to land in Mexico City, on the day Pres. Francisco Maduro was inaugurated. (COAM.)

BESSIE RAICHE. Inspired to take to the air by her husband, François, Wisconsin-born Bessie Raiche (1875–1932) was the first woman to fly a plane solo. After an earlier pilot, Blanche Stuart Scott, was disqualified from the distinction because her flight was deemed to be accidental in nature, Raiche claimed the title at the Hempstead Plains after lifting her plane, a homemade flyer, just a few feet off the ground. She and her husband founded the French-American Aeroplane Company, making and selling planes patterned after the model she flew.

BERNETTA A. MILLER. Born in Ohio, Bernetta Miller (1884–1972) was awarded the Croix de Guerre and was the fifth female pilot licensed in the United States. She, too, attended the Moisant Aviation School, where she took to the air in an impressive way from the start. During her test flights, which she did by moonlight, she rose to an altitude of 600 feet after being asked to rise only to 150, and landed her plane within 20 feet of a designated spot. In 1912, she demonstrated the efficacy of a Moisant-Bleriot airplane before the US Army at College Park in Maryland. She went on to say, "The Moisant [school] apparently calculated that I could overcome some of the fears others might have of the monoplane. I suppose that this was on the basis of the idea that if a mere woman could learn to fly one, so surely could a man."

FIRST AMERICAN AIRWOMAN

MISS QUIMBY FLIES WELL AND GETS HER DIPLOMA.

Sets Up a World's Record at Accurate Landing, Fulfils the Altitude Requirement and Cuts Figure Eights Like the Best of Them—Club May Take Her In.

Miss Harriet Quimby is the first American woman to hold an air diploma. She made her qualifying flights over the Hempstead Plains aviation field yesterday morning and in addition to fulfiling the requirement she set up a world's record for accurate landing. According to air rules the aviator must land within 164 feet of a designated spot. Her mark was 7 feet 9 inches.

Miss Quimby was out in her aerial toggery before 5 o'clock but was unable to get up before 7 o'clock on account of a heavy fog. By this time the sun had come out and the air was still. Miss Quimby mounted the seat of her monoplane without any sign of nervousness and quickly arose to a height of about 150 feet. She made a series of figure eights, which is considered one of the most difficult feats in flying because it calls for both the right and left turn. The course is indicated by two posts set about 1,600 feet apart and the loops of the figure are flown around the posts. An airman's degree calls for two uninterrupted series of these figure eights.

After completing the first series Miss Quimby made the record for accurate landing. She let the aero rest for a while to cool the motor and then she took wing again and completed the second series. This time she came down within 124 feet of the mark. On a third flight she tried for altitude, the required height being 164 feet. She went up 200 feet.

"Weren't you afraid?" some one asked this airwoman after she had landed.

"Not in the least," she replied. "I feel safer flying alone than when I go as a passenger. At the helm one has a sense of security that couldn't be had if another person is doing the driving. For several years I have driven an automobile, but I find more real pleasure in an aeroplane."

Miss Quimby said it is not her purpose to take up aviation as an occupation, but she will fly at all of the big meets. She intends to take part in the Chicago tournament that is to be held from August 8 to August 12. She was told by an official of the Aero Club of America yesterday that she may be made a member of that organization, which is now composed entirely of men. The matter will be taken up by the board of governors. They may form a woman's auxiliary. Miss Quimby was born in southern California. She has lived in New York for the last six years. With her parents she makes her home at the Victoria Hotel. She took up aviation last February and has made most of her flights between 4 and 5 o'clock in the morning, giving herself time to get to New York for business. She is employed on a magazine.

Ferdinand de Murias of Havana, Cuba, a pupil of the Moisant school, qualified yesterday as a pilot. While he was in the air George Beatty of the Wright school flew over from the Nassau Boulevard aerodrome to see the flights. In landing Beatty collided with a Moisant machine that was on the ground, breaking the rear rudder and damaging a wing of his own machine. Al Welch flew over when he heard of the wreck and carried Beatty back as a passenger.

"FIRST AMERICAN AIRWOMAN" HARRIET QUIMBY. A widely respected journalist and someone known for her elegance, Michigan native Harriet Quimby (1875–1912) decided to become an aviator soon after witnessing her first air show at Long Island's Belmont Park in 1910. She emerged from Hempstead's Moisant School as the first American woman to get a pilot's license (see article at left). Clad in her trademark purple satin flying costume, Quimby first took to barnstorming. Her flying career reached new heights in 1912, as she became the first woman to fly across the English Channel. But her career proved to be all too brief; in July 1912, at Boston's third annual aviation meet, while flying 2,000 feet over Dorchester Bay, Quimby lost control of her plane. She and her passenger were immediately killed when it struck the ground.

GLENN CURTISS: AVIATION GENIUS. After the Wright brothers' groundbreaking flight at Kitty Hawk in 1903, Glenn Curtiss (1878–1930) worked to realize the potential of powered flight. In 1907, he joined a group of like-minded individuals to form the Aerial Experiment Association, directed by Alexander Graham Bell. A master inventor, Curtiss designed and tested many of the association's airplanes, the first of which he flew at Hammondsport, New York, successfully flying his first plane, the *Gold Bug*, on July 4, 1909. Six days later, Curtiss moved his operations to the Hempstead Plains, where, among his accomplishments, he took off from Garden City's Washington Avenue airfield. Just a week later, to the delight of 2,500 spectators, he circled the field for nearly an hour in his *Golden Flyer* (below). Because he flew more than 25 kilometers, he was awarded $10,000 by *Scientific American*.

EARLE OVINGTON, BIRDMAN. The US post office came up with airmail service thanks to Earle Ovington (1879–1936). An aeronautical engineer, aviator, and inventor, Ovington piloted the first airmail flight in a rather artless affair. On September 23, 1911, while flying his Blériot XI *Dragonfly*, Ovington transported an official US mail sack from the Nassau Boulevard Aerodrome to a designated place in Mineola. After circling the area at 500 feet, he simply tossed the bag over the side of his plane. The sack broke open on impact and its contents scattered, one of which was a letter the post office sent to Ovington calling him "Official Air Mail Pilot No. 1." (The lesson he learned was to use a stronger sack next time.) Ovington's use of his plane was noteworthy enough to be reenacted 20 years later, with veteran pilot Dean Smith flying Ovington's exact route. (Below, COAM.)

AFRICAN AMERICAN ACE BESSIE COLEMAN. In the early 20th century, African Americans were not extended the opportunity to take part in any aspect of aviation, making the determination of Texas-born Bessie Coleman (1892–1926) to be the first to earn a pilot's license all the more remarkable. "Brave Bessie" soon made headlines by being the first black woman to fly in an airshow, at Curtiss Field, to honor veterans of the all-black 369th American Expeditionary Force of World War I. But she was better known for her barnstorming routines. Tragedy struck in 1926 as she tested a new plane she had just purchased and it went into an unexpected nosedive. As it descended, it flipped upside down, plunging Coleman to an untimely death. It is said that only the black-owned newspapers covered her death at the time, even though 10,000 mourners, led by activist Ida B. Wells, attended her funeral.

QUENTIN ROOSEVELT, WAR HERO, 1917. Smiling here is Lt. Quentin Roosevelt, Pres. Theodore Roosevelt's beloved son, who in the fall of 1917 was ordered to report to Issoudun, France. He was assigned to the 95th Pursuit Squadron and sent to the front in April 1918. That July, he was killed in air combat. Hazelhurst Field, where this picture was taken, was renamed Roosevelt Field in his honor. (GCVAC.)

R34 Dirigible At Roosevelt Field, July 1919. Apparent in this image is the sheer size of Britain's R34 dirigible at rest on Roosevelt Field after its historic flight to these shores. On July 2, the R34, under the command of Maj. George Scott, left Britain, arriving here 108 hours later on July 6, just as she was about to run out of fuel. As the personnel on the ground had no experience in helping land airships, one of its crew, Maj. John E.M. Pritchard, parachuted safely onto the field beneath him, making him the first airborne person from Europe to touch American soil. The R34's landing marked the first east-west aerial crossing of the Atlantic.

HAZELHURST FIELD (OR FIELD NO. 1), 1919. In this vivid aerial view facing northwest is a neat image of Hazelhurst Field. Shortly after this photograph was taken, Hazelhurst was split into two, with this portion (originally Aviation Field No. 1) soon renamed Roosevelt Field. (COAM.)

OPENING DAY, CURTISS FIELD, MAY 15, 1921. The excitement is palpable as Curtiss Field (seen here from a northeast perspective, looking toward the hangars along Old Country Road) is opening its gates to civilians, who, judging from the flood of cars parked for the occasion, were eager to catch a glimpse of pilots performing stunts in their Jennies. (GCVAC.)

SAD ARRIVAL, ROOSEVELT FIELD, APRIL 1928. Note the flurry of excitement near the Ford Trimotor plane at left. Its pilots, Floyd Bennett and Bernt Balchen, went to rescue three Bremen crew members stranded in Greely Island, Canada, after their nonstop flight from Germany. But Bennett had pneumonia, which worsened on the journey home. Balchen took the plane to Quebec to find medical care. Upon hearing of Bennett's condition, Charles Lindbergh flew through harsh conditions to Quebec to deliver a serum, but, as it turned out, the wrong kind. Bennett died of his illness and Balchen brought the plane home. (COAM.)

GOLD BUG HOTEL (FORMERLY F. MUNCH HOTEL), C. 1920s. On the northeast corner of Old Country Road and Willis Avenue, one block west of the Washington Avenue Field, was this humble stay-over for local aviators hoping to make good. (One such was Glenn Curtiss, who used it as his "Aeronautical Headquarters.") The hotel's beloved proprietor (standing in front) was Peter McLaughlin, who died in 1934. To pay homage to him, the *Roosevelt Field News* penned the following: "An old timer in aviation, seldom heard of in these later days but known to all the pioneers in the art of flying. . . . Peter F. McLaughlin, unsung as an air hero, made a great contribution to flying. Back in the early days when flying was little more than a dream, he saw the vision of aviation as it was to be, and with an interest and generosity that never left him throughout the years, gave a helping hand to the struggling unknowns who, with such help necessary, are responsible for a great part of the experimental work that gave aviation to the world."

ELINOR SMITH, DAREDEVIL, OCTOBER 22, 1928. Autumn in New York, Elinor Smith style: acting on a bet, Smith, who was just 17, flew her Waco 10 under all four of New York City's East River bridges, including the Manhattan Bridge seen here. (Unbeknownst to Smith, newsreel crews rushed to each bridge to catch her in flight.) She is the only pilot to have performed this astounding feat, and most assuredly the last. In what amounted to a slap on the wrist for the stunt, municipal authorities grounded her for 15 days. When the US Department of Commerce sought to suspend her license altogether, Mayor Jimmy Walker interceded on her behalf.

"BAD BOY" BERT ACOSTA. Most early aviators understood that to realize their full potential, abiding by rules was necessary. Others, however, like colorful Bert Acosta (1895–1954), seen here at the Curtiss factory in 1921, would flout them. In 1928, he had his license suspended for flying under Naugatuck's Whittemore Memorial Bridge as part of an advertising campaign for Splitdorf Spark Plugs. (Local legend has it that the wingspan of his plane exceeded the bridge's center arch, so he had to bank the plane to pass through.) A year later, he was fined for low flying and stunting—only to have his license revoked after he failed to pay the fine. In 1930, he was arrested in Connecticut for flying without a license. In 1931, he test flew a new Terle Sportplane to great fanfare at Roosevelt Field; the trouble was, he was still forbidden to fly, and the plane was unregistered. Despite his dubious reputation, Acosta went on to lead the Yankee Squadron during the Spanish Civil War, and in 2014 was posthumously inducted into the National Aviation Hall of Fame. (COAM.)

CHARLES J. DE BEVER AND TRANSMITTER, 1929. Equipped with a state-of-the-art transmitter that he would soon test in a parachute descent is parachute instructor Charles J. Debever at Roosevelt Field. Note the microphone strapped to his chin and the transmitter (then the smallest made) around his waist, which De Bever used to broadcast the experience of his descent through a network of NBC radio stations. The transmitter had a range of 10 miles, weighed 24 pounds, and ran on four batteries.

COMMANDER RICHARD E. BYRD, 1888–1957. When this photograph was taken in June 1927, Richard Byrd was the only man to fly to the North Pole. In the image below, his plane, dubbed the *America*, is officially christened at Roosevelt Field by relatives of department store magnate and aviation sponsor Rodman Wanamaker.

MISS AMERICA OF AVIATION, OCTOBER 1927. Months after Charles Lindbergh's historic flight to Paris in May 1927 came that of 23-year-old Ruth Elder (1902–1977), who is seen here waving on a runway at Roosevelt Field while boarding the *American Girl* that she would pilot to Paris. Accompanying her was navigator George Haldeman. As bad luck would have it, they were forced to land in the ocean 350 miles off the Azores after their oil tank ruptured. A Danish freighter came to their rescue.

ROOSEVELT FIELD WELCOMES HAROLD GATTY AND WILEY POST, 1931. Being interviewed in the midst of the crowd hailing their arrival at Roosevelt Field are Wiley Post (left) and Harold Gatty, intrepid air adventurers who, in the *Winnie Mae*, journeyed around the world (amounting to 16,000 miles) in eight and a half days, then a record-breaking time. Between the two men is news reporter Floyd Gibbons, who was well known for his fast-talking delivery on the radio, making him well-suited to capture the spirit of the moment.

KEYSTONE LB-6 BOMBERS, C. 1930S. A group of LB-6 bombers head from Roosevelt Field toward Mitchel Field. These 13,000-pound light bombers were built by the Keystone Air Company for the Army Air Corps starting in 1928. The LB-6 and its subsequent variants remained in operation until 1934. (COAM.)

"NAGIRROC YAW GNORW LIAH," JULY 1938. The *New York Post* ran this unique headline to honor newly-minted folk hero Douglas Corrigan after the aviator returned from his misdirected sojourn to Ireland, a fabled 28-hour trip that took place although he was supposed to fly to Long Beach, California. Some at the time contended that Corrigan's flight was intentional, after being denied permission to fly from New York to Dublin. Corrigan always maintained that this was not the case, that it was an honest mistake. This epic lapse notwithstanding, he was an experienced hand in aviation, being part of a team of mechanics who built Charles Lindbergh's *Spirit of St. Louis* (see pages 154–157). In this postcard, he sports a smile for the camera at Roosevelt Field.

GEORGE C. DADE. From a boy enamored with celebrity aviators taking off from his front lawn (Curtiss Field being his first childhood home) to an accomplished aviator in his own right, and later the keeper of aviation memory as the founder of the Cradle of Aviation Museum at Mitchel Field, it is safe to say that George Dade's passion for flight suffused every moment of his life. At 16, Dade became one of the youngest pilots to be licensed at the time. In this c. 1928 photograph, Dade (1913–1998) steps up to help Charles Lindbergh, the first in his long line heroes, adjust his parachute.

"THE LONE EAGLE" CHARLES AUGUSTUS LINDBERGH, 1927. Gazing at the camera is a self-assured Charles Lindbergh (1902–1974), standing before his beloved Ryan monoplane, the *Spirit of St. Louis*. Soon after this picture was taken, he would embark from Roosevelt Field for his historic transatlantic flight on May 20, 1927, to claim the $10,000 Orteig prize that came with it. To historian Joshua Stoff, Lindbergh "was young and of an 'all-American' type" but known for his reticent, even solitary, nature. While nurturing his dream to take to the sky, Lindbergh studied the latest scientific developments on aviation; it is said that the *Spirit of St. Louis* was the best-suited plane technologically for his epic flight. "More than any other single flight since the Wright brothers," Stoff said, "Lindbergh's triumph revolutionized aviation. . . . [His flight] enhanced the credibility of the civilian pilot and demonstrated the enormous potential of aviation." After he landed in Le Bourget Field near Paris, 33.5 hours after he left American soil, Lindbergh was met with throngs of cheering people. He did not anticipate such a greeting. Also extending a welcoming hand was history itself.

BEFORE THE EPIC FLIGHT, MAY 1927. Lindbergh patiently waited for days at the nearby Garden City Hotel for a spell of inclement weather to clear so he could embark on his groundbreaking flight. The *Spirit of St. Louis* was originally stored in a hangar at Curtiss Field, but in the early morning on May 20, Lindbergh had it moved to Roosevelt Field slightly to the east because he preferred its longer runway. This undated photograph shows Lindbergh heading toward the *Spirit of St. Louis* as it is wheeled into its hangar, or possibly being pulled out. Maybe he is disappointed that he could not take off; notice the puddle, indicating recent rain. But the prevailing mood here will never be known. This is a tantalizing photograph for sure.

MAY 20, 1927. Taken by a reporter, the photograph above of Roosevelt Field shows a crowd of well-wishers and press surrounding the *Spirit of St. Louis* moments before Lindbergh embarked on his transatlantic flight. The mood was tense with excitement. As Stoff put it, "At 7:52 a.m., Lindbergh headed his silver monoplane eastward down the muddy mile-long highway, heavily loaded with 2,750 pounds of fuel (slightly more than the aircraft had been designed to take off with). At liftoff, he barely cleared the trees at the end of the runway. Once Lindbergh was aloft, the entire country prayed for him. . . . The 'Lone Eagle' was heading into the unknown." The photograph below shows the *Spirit of St. Louis* as it left Roosevelt Field.

MAKING HISTORY 33.5 HOURS LATER, MAY 21, 1927. After an exhausting flight, Lindbergh reached his destination at 10:22 p.m. local time. Much to his amazement, over 100,000 ecstatic Parisians swarmed to the *Spirit of St. Louis* to greet him and to catch a glimpse of history in the form of a hero whose pioneering spirit transcended all boundaries. According to Joshua Stoff, Lindbergh was utterly astonished to witness the cheering multitude calling for him, as he figured no one would meet him to begin with. Such was the modesty that made the man. With his flight, the Old and the New Worlds embraced each other in an unprecedented way. In this instance, representing the New World was Roosevelt Field. (GCVAC.)

AFTERWORD

Today, the Stewart legacy finds itself under a continual stress test.

While their contemporaries solidified their legacies through acts of civic consciousness, the Stewarts' creation of Garden City had an air of divine inspiration. As such, Alexander and Cornelia thought their community would last for ages.

Then came the challenges of modernity. A critical point came with the Garden City Hotel's demolition in 1973, an act that led to a successful effort to protect the area's remaining historically important structures. Another hotel (the fourth) emerged from the rubble, yet sadly, other than its shape and dimensions, little of its predecessor's architectural distinction is evident.

The tragic loss of St. Mary's school in 2000 looms over the fate of its counterpart: the St. Paul's school. Despite being listed in the National Register of Historic Places, questions over its rehabilitation's expense persist. Once more, the Stewart legacy hangs in the balance.

In 2013, eight years after plaintiffs sued the village of Garden City over exclusionary housing practices, the Federal District Court found that the village "acted with discriminatory intent" in its violation of the Fair Housing Standards Act of 1965. The US Court of Appeals for the Second Circuit affirmed the lower court's decision. Yet village officials successfully waited out the clock, as the property in question will now be the site of Nassau County's new family court building. Where was the moral vision of the Stewarts in all this?

When it comes to Garden City, the past is prologue. From a utopian community to a paragon of Long Island suburbia, from stationing American soldiers in its midst to its place in aviation history, Garden City has long put the human experience on display. If our readers leave with that impression, the authors would be satisfied. Call it *our* legacy.

A REASON FOR SADNESS, 1973. In 1971, financial difficulties forced the third Garden City Hotel to close; two years later, amid a play of "Taps" and before 200 spectators bidding farewell, it had a fateful rendezvous with history. A three-ton wrecking ball tore down what was (with due deference to the Cathedral of the Incarnation) the defining feature of the Garden City community. There was a promise that "proper" development would be made, and with the current hotel, a case can be made that it has. However, although the local landscape has healed somewhat, never again will it "feel" like it did before. Whether the present hotel will become as historically important as its predecessor is something only time—an abundance of it—will tell. (GCVAC.)

BIBLIOGRAPHY

Czachowski, Joe. *Historic Photos of Long Island*. Nashville, TN: Turner Publishing Company, 2009.

Dade, George C. and Frank Strnad. *Picture History of Aviation on Long Island 1908–1938*. New York, NY: Dover Publications, 1989.

Davis, John W. *Dominion in the Sea: History of the Diocese of Long Island*. Hempstead, NY: Georgin Foundation, 1977.

Elias, Stephen N. *Alexander T. Stewart: The Forgotten Merchant Prince*. Westport, CT: Praeger Publishers, 1992.

Kordes, John Ellis. *Visions of Garden City* (second ed.). Garden City, NY: self-published, 2007.

McKenna, James M. "Nassau County's Camp Mills in the Great War, 1917–1918." *Nassau County Historical Journal* 73 (2018): 26–38.

Monti, Gary. "Mitchel Air Force Base on the Hempstead Plains" *Nassau County Historical Journal* 73 (2018): 39–45.

Panchyk, Richard. *Hempstead Plains from Above*. Charleston, SC: Arcadia Publishing, 2020.

Smith, M.H. *Garden City, Long Island, in Early Photographs: 1869–1919*. New York, NY: Dover Publications, 1987.

————. *History of Garden City* (revised ed.). New York, NY: Garden City Historical Society, 1980.

Stoff, Joshua. *Charles A. Lindbergh: The Life of the "Lone Eagle" in Photographs*. Mineola, NY: Dover Publications, 1995.

Seyfried, Vincent. *The Founding of Garden City*. Special Centennial Edition. Uniondale, NY: Salisbury Printers, 1969.

van Wie, Paul D. *Landmarks of Hempstead Town*. New York, NY: Franklin Square Historical Society, 2016.

Vollono, Millicent D. and Lauren V. Drapala. "Designing Suburbia: Olive Tjaden on Long Island." *Nassau County Historical Journal* 71 (2016): 1–14.

Welch, Richard F. *Long Island and World War I*. Charleston, SC: The History Press, 2018.

Welch, Rosanne. *Encyclopedia of Women in Aviation and Space*. Santa Barbara, CA: ABC-CLIO Inc., 1998

DISCOVER THOUSANDS OF LOCAL HISTORY BOOKS FEATURING MILLIONS OF VINTAGE IMAGES

Arcadia Publishing, the leading local history publisher in the United States, is committed to making history accessible and meaningful through publishing books that celebrate and preserve the heritage of America's people and places.

Find more books like this at
www.arcadiapublishing.com

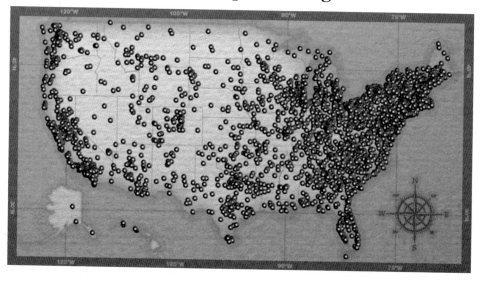

Search for your hometown history, your old stomping grounds, and even your favorite sports team.